Praise for *Insic*

CW01558359

"A tremendous resource, amalgamating c(
that is presented in a concise, easy to
Shareholder, Akerman Senterfitt

"Aspatore's *Inside the Minds* series allows strategic professionals to access cutting-edge information from proven experts in the field. Their approach of providing consolidated, valuable, current information reflects their true understanding of the life of an executive. We need the best information in the most concise format. Aspatore is a consistently reliable resource that provides great information without expending unnecessary time." – Kimberly L. Giangrande, Principal, Intuitive HR

"A terrific compilation of real world, successful strategies and practical advice."
– Sig Anderman, CEO, Ellie Mae Inc.

"Must read source for leaders wanting to stay ahead of emerging best practices and to understand the thought processes leading up to the innovation." – Mark Gasta, SVP and Chief Human Resources Officer, Vail Resorts Management Company

"A refreshing collection of strategic insights, not dreary commonplaces, from some of the best of the profession." – Roger J. Magnuson, Partner, Dorsey & Whitney LLP

"Unique and insightful perspectives. Great to read and an excellent way to stay in touch. – Filippo Passerini, President of Global Business Services and CIO, The Procter & Gamble Company

"A must read for C-level and senior executives. The information is based on actual experiences from successful senior leaders and has real, practical value presented in a very useable format." – Stephen Fugale, VP and CIO, Villanova University

"Some of the best insight around from sources in the know" – Donald R. Kirk, Shareholder, Fowler White Boggs PA

"Powerful insight from people who practice every day!" – Andrea R. Bortner, VP, GCSD Human Resources, Harris Corporation

"Aspatore's *Inside the Minds* series provides practical, cutting edge advice from those with insight into the real world challenges that confront businesses in the global economy." – Michael Bednarek, Partner, Shearman & Sterling LLP

"Outstanding insights from respected business leaders." – R. Scot Sellers, CEO, Archstone

ASPATORE

www.Aspatore.com

Aspatore Books, a Thomson Reuters business, exclusively publishes C-Level executives (CEO, CFO, CTO, CMO, Partner) from the world's most respected companies and law firms. C-Level Business Intelligence™, as conceptualized and developed by Aspatore Books, provides professionals of all levels with proven business intelligence from industry insiders—direct and unfiltered insight from those who know it best—as opposed to third-party accounts offered by unknown authors and analysts. Aspatore Books is committed to publishing an innovative line of business and legal books, those which lay forth principles and offer insights that when employed, can have a direct financial impact on the reader's business objectives. In essence, Aspatore publishes critical tools for all business professionals.

Inside the Minds

The *Inside the Minds* series provides readers of all levels with proven legal and business intelligence from C-Level executives and lawyers (CEO, CFO, CTO, CMO, Partner) from the world's most respected companies and law firms. Each chapter is comparable to a white paper or essay and is a future-oriented look at where an industry, profession, or topic is heading and the most important issues for future success. Each author has been selected based upon their experience and C-Level standing within the professional community. *Inside the Minds* was conceived in order to give readers actual insights into the leading minds of top lawyers and business executives worldwide, presenting an unprecedented look at various industries and professions.

INSIDE THE MINDS

CEO Leadership Strategies

Leading CEOs on Driving Accountability,
Managing Change, and Fostering Growth

ASPATORE

CONTENTS

The Art of Authentic Leadership

Kevin J. Kennedy
President and Chief Executive Officer
Avaya

ASPATORE

Introduction

I have been chief executive officer (CEO) of Avaya for eighteen months. Because this company is transitioning from one generation of technology to the next, our primary goals are to make sure we improve our business model, find the right talent to perform the tactical execution work that is required, and then develop the right strategies that will enable us to reinvent our product portfolio.

Avaya is unique within our industry in a number of ways. First, we're proud that, for the past four years, we've been named by the Ethisphere Institute one of the world's most ethical companies. Second, we are one of the few companies in the business-to-business communications space that is in the $4 billion to $5 billion range. Ours is an industry of polarities, to some degree. There are the many that are in the $1 billion to $2 billion category, and then there are the Ciscos and Microsofts of the world, that are $50 billion to $100 billion. We are distinctive in terms of our size. Finally, our offering a mix of roughly 50 percent product and 50 percent services defines an exceptional business model.

Avaya has good recognition in the industry analysts' community, where we spend substantial time. We are one of only three suppliers named a Leader in Gartner Magic Quadrant for Unified Communications. We are also in the Leaders' Quadrant for Corporate Telephony and Contact Center Infrastructure. But I don't think marketing has been one of our strengths over the last several years, and we could definitely improve in this area. However, I actually think private companies do sometimes suffer from lack of brand recognition because they don't have a ticker number that people see on TV every day.

The earlier heyday of the enterprise communications business occurred in a product market that was called the private branch exchange (PBX), which basically supported business-to-business phone and messaging services. Architecturally these products have now evolved to provide the same functions in ways that are more software- than hardware-based. Of course, modes of communication have expanded from exclusively voice to video, data, etc., as well as voice. We're in the midst of transitioning an older technology that has lasted for many decades to support a new world of collaboration that will transform the way people interact within the enterprise. In sum, collaboration is the new piece of our evolution.

The CEO's Role in Reinventing the Company

As I've led the company through this transformation, I don't believe my role as CEO has changed much. The "evolution" was in how I as a new leader came into this asset and gained alignment with the many stakeholders with whom we interact and on whom we depend. This includes employees, customers, partners, the board of directors, and so forth.

One blessing was that I had actually worked in this part of the business years ago, back when it was the enterprise communications division of AT&T and then Lucent Technologies. The division was spun out of Lucent in late 2000 to become the independent company known as Avaya, and I joined the company as CEO in January 2009. At some level, my experience is akin to that of a child who returns home, although the home may have been significantly remodeled and redecorated.

We weathered the recession quite well, continuing to generate cash. Consequently, from a board perspective, the leadership team was deemed competent to manage the profit and loss of the company, as well as the cash cycle of the company. This year we brought an unprecedented number of new products to market, so I think our customers are watching us become more relevant. These are all good developments, and, as they represent changes from the past, they can be considered a sort of evolution in my and the company's interactions with some of the key stakeholder groups.

However, leaders must be able to adapt constantly so that they are always positioned to solve the most pressing problems of their companies. If you don't respond to changes in the marketplace, you will be left behind. The environment is changing faster today than ever, so every company needs to aspire to responding quickly to new conditions. Consequently, I think being fast is important. I'd say this company is improving in that respect.

As a company matures and begins to focus on executing new models, leaders, including CEOs, feel an urgency to spend more and more time with customers. Leaders who get out and talk to customers will see themes they can bring back to their teams for discussion and digestion. The key point here is if you're talking to your customers, you're always becoming aware of problems they're trying to solve—independent of whether the solutions they are selecting in the moment are correct. Nothing takes the place of getting out there and listening to the marketplace—and doing it frequently. That helps you be agile.

If any aspect of my role will change in the coming years, it will probably be in how I use my time. I hope I will be able to continue to increase the amount of time available to look outward.

Definition of an "Authentic" Leadership Style

Concerning my leadership style, I'd say I'm known to be fairly authentic and direct, and I enjoy a high level of operational engagement. I tend to do things deliberately and have a method for accessing the pulse of various activities in the company. This involves setting up a disciplined cadence of meetings and reviews with both my team and other employees to monitor the metrics of the business.

Because during any quarter, certain issues will need special attention, being able to do triage is an important skill. I don't need to spend disproportionate amounts of time with staff who are not actively involved in these issues. I figure out the biggest blocking issues of the quarter and then spend more time with the people who are most likely to be able to solve those problems. When it comes to people, issues, and tactics, I tend to "manage by exception"—i.e., concentrate my time where the problems are, rather than democratically or uncritically granting access across the board. I prioritize to make sure my time is used as effectively as possible.

However, I also start with a point of view on where the industry is evolving, and consequently I devote a fair amount of time to the strategy of the company. In summation, I would say I'm strongly driven by process on the operational front and interested, curious, and engaged on the strategy front.

Setting and Meeting Goals for the Year

Each year we start with the strategy and then determine which actions are required to execute the strategy. Next we figure out who is accountable, what the top priorities are, and where we draw the line on the priorities. In any year, there are usually more than three and fewer than ten priorities, so I assess which are most likely to move forward without my immediate effort and which will need more help. We constantly test directions, priorities, etc., with customers. That means communicating where we are investing, why, and seeking feedback from customers weekly. In this way, we establish the priorities for the company, as well as identify those that will need my personal attention.

Each quarter and at the beginning of the fiscal year, we present those priorities to the board and garner their feedback, support, and endorsement. At this point, we also share them with employees and invite their feedback. In addition, I usually have three somewhat formalized calls per quarter (one per month) with the board to discuss financial results. Then I relay status checks roughly twice per quarter through e-mail or informal calls with the board and the chairman on special topics or updates. So, relative to some public companies, we maintain a fairly rigorous schedule of communications with our seven-member board to ensure our goals remain aligned. Because we're private, the board members are also owners of the company.

To track progress toward our plans and priorities, we have monthly meetings in which my direct reports formally present the status of their functions to their peers and me. This is self-reporting. Once per quarter we hold deeper discussions in which we assess whether our strategy continues to be correct. I also tend to meet separately with each of my direct reports at least twice a month to make sure they are progressing or see whether I can help them remove bottlenecks. We use a standardized format that covers customers, results, new opportunities, risks, and so forth. Approximately ten items are included in the agenda so we can be sure we are addressing the most important things.

In total, our conversations about progress occur anywhere from weekly to bi-weekly and formally every month. If we were to entertain discussion on every activity, risk, opportunity, and initiative under way in the business, not only would we spend our lives in meetings, but we also would surely be scattered and unfocused in our execution. Limiting the topics to ten prevents that from happening.

If something isn't progressing according to plan, we will also schedule out-of-cycle "exception meetings." In addition, I'm a fan of open-door interactions, whether I'm dropping in on someone, or others see my open door and stop by. By holding both one-on-one meetings and meetings in the round, I see the company and each function through multiple lenses. These varying perspectives enable me to ask better questions. Also, because I tend to know what's going on, I can stay fairly well-focused on execution and, in turn, can serve as a mirror to allow people to see what is happening. Keeping myself well informed helps me avoid leading in a dogmatic, opinionated way.

Communicating across the Company

We try to meet virtually with all employees every four to six weeks and give e-mail updates every couple of weeks. Soon we will embark on a schedule of bi-weekly communications on three areas that are important to me. One is customer intimacy. The second is lean productivity improvement. And the third is innovation. We will pick three teams that will give these updates every other week to our employee base: What are we learning in each of the three areas and how are we succeeding? I've picked them because I think all three are crucial to guiding us into our future and helping our employee base celebrate some of the good things that are happening on those three fronts. I think this emphasis serves as a reminder about what's important.

In addition, I try to hold small, cross-functional, skip-level meetings, breakfasts, and roundtables at least once per month in our headquarters location and whenever I am visiting an employee location outside headquarters. I also maintain a separate e-mailbox where employees can send questions and comments or share good news, which we then find opportunities to publicize more broadly.

In summation, our leadership team and employee meetings are probably the two most important ways we keep company stakeholders aligned with company priorities and execution. In addition, we obviously have many marketing campaigns through customers and channel partners, but I'd say my time is mostly invested in employee and board-level communications.

Avaya: One of America's Most Ethical Companies

Our designation by Ethisphere Institute as one of the most ethical companies was driven largely by our chief administrative officer and general counsel, Pam Craven. She has helped us set a tone and level of training and engagement that turns intent into actions.

The basis of our recognition as an ethical company is the way we train every new employee on what ethical behavior is and how to identify situations that should be avoided. Not only do we train people by generating awareness, but also we actually conduct required tests that assess our employees' capacity to exercise the right judgment.

Our level of training and testing in this area differentiate us from many other companies. The hours that are devoted to this training and testing are quite significant. In some companies, employees would consider this burdensome. But it's a commitment we've made; we make every effort to reinforce it through "tone at the top"; and we continue to hope this level of attention will result in a workforce that will make the right judgments.

Motivating the Workforce in a Turnaround Situation: Successes and Challenges

Motivating a workforce can be difficult when the company is going through a turnaround. We recently bought a large division of Nortel Networks Corporation, Nortel Enterprise Solutions. As in many merger and acquisition (M&A) situations, it required some headcount reduction. Any time this happens, there will be a natural ebbing effect on people's enthusiasm.

However, to motivate people as much as we can, we first emphasize that our business is growing and doing well. We try to encourage them to look in the right direction and through the right door. Second, we share that this year will probably be the most significant one we've experienced in a decade in terms of the innovations we've brought to the market. We're putting a heavy emphasis on how we're reinventing the company and going into new markets, which should serve us well for growth in the future. Third, we have invested in identifying a fairly sizeable number of new leaders who, we think, have the energy, insight, and inspiration to be better leaders going forward. Finally, I think we're beginning to have more complete and transparent conversations with people so that they don't feel orphaned as we change. We are also holding supervisors accountable for conducting regular and meaningful performance conversations, not only at midyear and year-end, but also on an ongoing basis. While these good practices are not unusual, we are engaging in them now with more intensity.

However, doing turnarounds is difficult because ultimately you're trying to reinvent the company. To oversimplify a bit, because market changes have occurred, you're making the company different than it was before, and this is just not easy operationally or emotionally. One hard reality is that, in this process, you are usually taking one or two steps forward and then a step back. The key is to keep putting one foot in front of the other. Operationally there is an intense need to "open the door" to the future, where the growth is, get people *aligned,* and have them grab it, so that they can let go and transition from the past. This is hard work, and everyone moves at a different speed.

Example of a Specific Leadership Challenge

Probably one of the greatest leadership challenges I had was in my last job as the CEO of JDS Uniphase during the period when we faced a shareholder lawsuit (which predated my start as the CEO). We were being sued for $20 billion at a time when we had a market capitalization of around $3 billion to $3.5 billion, so the shareholder lawsuit represented potential bankruptcy of the company. The leadership challenge occurred not just because of the drama of the potential outcome but also, as a CEO who's an engineer trying to lead a board through a drama like that, I didn't come with any particular stature—in fact, probably the reverse. Because I wasn't a lawyer, my opinion was no more relevant (and in fact probably less relevant) than those of many of the board members.

The conventional wisdom for surviving such a process, which takes a long time, is that you just settle, independent of the facts, because it's less distraction, and you get it over with. Out of 2,150 generally similar shareholder lawsuits, up to that time, ours was the only case that actually went to trial, so you can appreciate that we were pursuing an unconventional course. Newspaper articles basically said JDS Uniphase was on the brink; the CEO must be nuts, and so forth. However, we kept the conversation alive. We brought in the experts, communicated with the board during the trial, and met every other day on a teleconference. We stayed the course. And we won. We were found innocent on all fifty-five counts.

During this whole ordeal, there was a moment when the board wanted to settle, but I did not believe that was the right thing. However, we were able to resolve that disconnect and return to alignment without damaging key relationships.

My point here is that when you're dealing in an area where you're not an expert, process is your friend. Process can help reveal the possibilities, rather than close doors. However, you do need to realize that, even if you do the right thing, you will not make everyone happy. This lawsuit involved a long process, but it was a critically important learning exercise for how to keep people aligned when you don't bring a natural knowledge to the table—and when not everyone will be happy with the result.

Advice for Upcoming CEOs

The 1990s was a better time to be a CEO than the 2000s because it's always better to run a company in an up market than during recessionary times. However, in all times, upcoming executives truly need to want to be CEOs because it's enormous work, and it can be lonely. But it is one of the few jobs where you can create a sense of culture and bring great people who you think will produce a particular outcome. If you enjoy bringing people together to form this collaborative culture, as well as pursue an outcome, this is a uniquely satisfying job. If you're doing it for any other reason, it becomes a pretty tough job.

Key Takeaways

- Organizations are living organisms, with personalities, intellectual capacities, emotional fragilities, and symptomatic health issues. That is why oversimplified or romanticized models of organizational behavior rarely work. Doing things deliberately, including maintaining a disciplined cadence of meetings, reviews, and interactions, helps leaders keep a realistic perspective on activities in the business.

- Leaders must aggressively set and stick to key priorities. Otherwise, the sheer surge of business and multiplicity of demands will sap leaders' energy and undermine their effectiveness.

- Our primary goals are to improve our business model, find the right talent to attain this model, and develop the right strategies that will enable us to reinvent our product portfolio.

- Leadership is hard and requires courage and tenacity. Most turnarounds and other difficult business transitions are marathons, not sprints. You are usually taking one or two steps forward and then a step back. The key is to keep putting one foot in front of the other.

- One-on-one meetings—both formal and informal—and meetings in the round help me see the company and each function through multiple lenses. These varying perspectives enable me to ask better questions.

- Our four best practices for motivating employees during tough transitions are: (1) emphasize where the business is growing and doing well; (2) share stories about the success that innovations have brought; (3) invest in future company leaders; and (4) communicate openly with employees about company changes. Trust is earned every day and can be eroded in a moment.

Kevin J. Kennedy is the president and chief executive officer (CEO) of Avaya, a leading global provider of business communications applications, systems, and services.

Prior to joining the company in January 2009, Mr. Kennedy served as president and CEO of JDS Uniphase Corporation, a position he had held since September 2003. He had also served as a member of the JDSU board of directors since November 2001.

Before joining JDSU, Mr. Kennedy served as chief operating officer of Openwave Systems Inc., a position he held from August 2001 to September 2003. Prior to joining Openwave Systems, he spent close to eight years at Cisco Systems Inc., most recently as senior vice president of the Service Provider Line of Business and Software Technologies Division.

Earlier in his career, Mr. Kennedy spent seventeen years with AT&T Bell Laboratories, serving in a number of assignments in the Lincroft, Holmdel, and Middletown, New Jersey, locations. During his Bell Labs tenure, he also lived and worked in Columbus, Ohio, as part of the Conversant voice information system team, in the AUDIX Voice Messaging organization.

In 1987, Mr. Kennedy was a congressional fellow to the U.S. House of Representatives Committee on Science, Space, and Technology. He was a member of the board of directors of Polycom Inc. until January 2009. He currently serves on the board of directors of KLA-Tencor Corporation and is a member of the board of regents of Loyola Marymount University.

Mr. Kennedy holds a BS in engineering from Lehigh University in Pennsylvania, as well as MS and PhD degrees in engineering from Rutgers University. He was an adjunct professor at Rutgers from 1982 to 1984 and has published more than thirty papers on computational methods, data networking, and issues of technology management.

In 2006, Mr. Kennedy was honored by the School of Engineering at Rutgers as its Alumnus of the Year and awarded an Alumni Medal of Excellence. He is a co-author of Going the Distance: Why Some Companies Dominate and Others Fail, *published in 2003.*

Driving Accountability and Performance across a Flat Organization

Erik Olsson
President and Chief Executive Officer
RSC Holdings

ASPATORE

Introduction: Evolution of the CEO Role

I am president and chief executive officer (CEO) of RSC Holdings Inc., the parent company of RSC Equipment Rental. I am also a director on the board. RSC is a public company listed on the NYSE under the ticker RRR.

Previously, I was with Atlas Copco, a global manufacturer, for approximately eighteen years. Atlas Copco owned RSC for a period of time, and that's how I came into the business. My manufacturing background gave me a unique perspective on the equipment rental business and has been the foundation for RSC's transformation.

RSC rents equipment and provides maintenance and support services to approximately 300,000 industrial and non-residential construction businesses across North America. We have more than 450 stores and 4,200 employees. In addition to being one of the largest companies in this sector, we're considered the industry leader.

I joined RSC in 2001 and was named CEO in 2006. My role at the company has evolved through a number of phases. When I first came to RSC, we were focused on effectively structuring the company, establishing strategy and processes, and stabilizing operations to build a strong, profitable foundation.

The second phase was all about growing the company; for me, personally, it was also to become a growth leader—i.e., to switch from cost-cutting and defense to driving sales and offense. The industry's weak customer service standard was a point of entry for us. We became a customer-centric organization and positioned RSC as an ideal partner to those customers seeking value, productivity, and low total cost (as opposed to low price and low quality, which drives higher costs for the customer). We began using the Net Promoter Score® (a survey of how likely customers are to recommend a company to a friend or colleague) to benchmark customer satisfaction. I am proud of our track record. Our customer satisfaction scores have improved every year. We now rank in the high sixties, among leading world-class service companies.

In the third and most recent phase, we devised a strategy to manage through the recession—we got back to basics and right-sized the company again, focusing on process and efficiency. However, we were conscious not to compromise what we achieved in phases one and two.

Going into the downturn, we were realizing the highest profit margins in the industry; this proved significant to how we addressed the recessionary environment. The profit margins and corresponding strong free cash flows enabled us to extend our focus beyond immediate market concerns of cost-cutting to also include strategies to strengthen the business for a recovery and long-term performance. Accordingly, we continued to invest heavily in the business, our fleet, and store footprint. We moved forward while our competitors struggled. As a result, we are back in the growth phase, stronger and better-positioned than before the recession.

It has been helpful for me to have seen the company through these distinct phases and to know what to expect and what to do in different environments.

When I became CEO, my first imprint on the strategy was to focus our organization's mindset on safety. You can't exercise credible leadership in an organization like RSC without making the environment safe for employees, customers, and the communities in which we operate. Safety is a point of differentiation in the equipment rental industry. It speaks to the quality of training, level of focus, and customer service. I am pleased that our safety metrics have dramatically improved. RSC is now the safest company in the industry.

Simultaneously I made an important strategic shift to reduce our dependence on the construction industry and diversify our revenues. Industrials were an attractive opportunity—they were less cyclical than construction, and the period of customer engagements were more consistent and long-term. I felt strongly that we could deepen RSC's reach in the industrial segment. My manufacturing background gave me great insights about how decision-makers at industrial companies function and make use of resources. Equipment was not a primary focus of these customers. Keeping their production process efficient and productive was their primary objective. I understood that if we could help customers focus on productivity, we would also benefit and become a business partner. This informed our industrial strategy and enhanced our people's ability to attract and serve these accounts.

We developed a highly compelling value proposition for the industrial market by building a sales team with direct industrial experience and tailoring services to meet our customers' needs. We offered equipment and tools for repair- and maintenance-related projects. Our services and inventory management software helped them reduce costs significantly. When we saw the downturn coming, we anticipated a rise in maintenance and repair demands and increased our service offering. These initiatives struck a chord with industrial customers and expanded our relationships beyond equipment rental. Now, as the industrial market rebounds faster and stronger than the construction market, it's great to see that this strategy continues to work for us. We're showing the industrial sector that we speak the same language; as a result, they may prefer to do business with RSC over one of our competitors.

An Open and Transparent Leadership Style

My leadership style is steeped in transparency and open communication. Over the years, I've learned that the more information you share, the better decisions the company makes—and these decisions can be made deeply in the organization if people have the information they need. Some think that information is power you should hold onto, but I'm on the opposite side of the spectrum: you should share as much as possible, thereby increasing the speed and quality of decision-making.

Ultimately, at RSC, it is about serving the customer. When dealing with customers, RSC employees have complete access to information and the authority to make immediate decisions. This is a positive experience for our customers—they want timely and efficient answers. As a result, our customer service and satisfaction levels are the industry's highest.

I find that transparency and open communication build credibility around our strategies and reinforce our corporate culture, fostering trust throughout the organization. To sustain this, you need to communicate over and over and over again. Doing so in person demonstrates that you are direct about things good and bad. At RSC, it is also the most effective way to discuss strategies or initiatives with our people. As part of this, I believe you must be highly involved in the business, and I require this of all my colleagues deep into the organization, regardless of position or function. It is imperative for all of our employees to fully understand what's going on in all parts of our business and what drives the right behavior and the desired performance at RSC.

We have a flat organization at RSC, which further underscores the need for open communication and transparency. My executive team and I spend a good portion of our time in the field, either in stores or with customers. This helps us understand what's going on so we can take corrective action when needed. Our presence in the field also conveys to our employees that the company leadership is truly engaged, and our actions are based on firsthand knowledge and facts. In addition, when our customers see the CEO or senior vice presidents (VPs) of the company on their job sites asking how we can do more to help them, they feel our company is a credible organization and business partner. I think that's another important piece of my leadership style.

In essence, it is important to establish a leadership platform that's characterized by transparency, openness, communication, and a deep understanding of the business. This is what leaders need to be truly effective.

Working as a Team with the C-level Executives

Transparency influences how I work with my C-level executives. I believe in keeping an operating rhythm in sharing relevant and current information with my C-level executives. We hold bi-weekly executive management meetings, and every Friday morning we have a call with the broader management team. We're organized into ten regions across the United States and Canada, and these calls are vital to our performance. During these calls, we ask the regional vice presidents, their sales managers, finance directors, and so on to spend ten minutes each sharing what's happened in their region that week and what the outlook is for the next week. Did they win any big accounts? Does somebody need help with something? Getting everyone on the phone at the same time is a great way to share information, reinforce the team building, and set direction.

Most companies do annual performance assessments, as we do. However, I have found that this is far too infrequent if you want to create and maintain a performance-driven culture. Instead, I meet with my senior team members every quarter to conduct performance reviews, follow up on goals, and lay out new objectives for the next quarter. I also use these meetings to solicit feedback on my performance from my direct reports. This is always helpful and again supports the type of open leadership style I encourage. I believe in doing 360s, but I don't think that's something you need to do every year—every third year is probably enough, even though that process is also extremely helpful and eye-opening.

I often travel with one of my senior team members; it's a good opportunity to catch up on things and to do some one-on-one coaching. Coaching is a big part of my leadership style. It relates to being open and transparent; everyone, including the senior team and me, can improve or think about things in new ways. Coaching, however, need not be very formal. Whenever I get an opportunity, I'll coach people at any level in the organization. I think coaching is a great way for me to both spread ideas I think are important and give recognition to people. When I make a point to sit and talk with them, they see that I have a vested interest in them. It underscores that they are important to the team.

Rather than tell people what to do, I suggest things they should think about or improvements they could make. I explain why they need to make a certain change or why they should think about doing things differently. Our exchange becomes an opportunity for the employee to engage and learn. I think this helps the employee and the company going forward.

Transparency Drives Accountability

To maintain a good operating rhythm, we track and evaluate critical areas of our business every day. As a numbers-driven organization, we work with a wealth of data and have built robust systems that support every level of our company with pertinent information. Every morning we assess numbers on sales, pricing, utilization, and fleet out on rent from the previous day, and we do this down to the branch level. This means we have a clear view of what is going on and who is accountable. By constantly looking at such information, we can discern problems or issues quickly.

Financial numbers are like a dairy product—they are fresh for only a couple of days. Looking at last month's numbers when you're two weeks into the new month is completely meaningless. I've always implemented routines and processes that enable us to close the books quickly. In line with keeping up this operating rhythm, we have the company's complete profit-and-loss sheet (P&L), balance sheets, and cash flows on the second day of every new month. This includes individual P&Ls for the divisions, the regions, and all of our 450 locations. We always have a good grip on what's going on in real-time and can focus on the new month ahead of us.

Accountability is a significant cornerstone of our decentralized business model. We delegate much of the decision-making and responsibilities down into the organization. To make that work, we use our systems, data, and exception reports to hold people accountable for their decisions. It also enables us to take corrective actions should something go wrong.

To further support our decentralized model and, especially, to get closer to our customers, we created relatively small spans of control in the field. Our 450 stores are divided over seventy-five districts, each with a district manager who oversees six to eight stores. This means he or she can visit each store weekly and make sure the right things are being done by our employees. The visits also allow for meetings with customers. We used to have only forty districts, but by breaking this span of control into smaller pieces, we can more directly ensure accountability in each territory.

As I've mentioned, we generate a great deal of information about the business from each location. On any given morning, I can sit at my screen and analyze specific store performance. I can see how it is doing with utilization or revenues and other related issues. This information is also accessible to employees across the entire organization. Store A can see how store B is doing and so on. I find internal competition to be a great motivator.

RSC's management structure is transparent; because we can see where responsibilities lie, people are always accountable for their performance. It's not unusual for me to pick up the phone and call a district manager or even a store manager and say, "Hey, I see this on the screen. What's going on?" I do this not only to learn about a particular detail, but also to emphasize to the manager that he or she is accountable for the work, and I see it, too. People appreciate being seen, even if it's not always when there's good news.

Developing and Motivating Employees

We believe employee education and training, regardless of position or title, are critical to company performance. Our universal training program is designed to strengthen the leadership, product, and general business knowledge of all employees. We have a training center in Denver where we do both sales and leadership training, and we are in the process of introducing more individual programs to our high-potentials and senior leaders. We place substantial emphasis on safety training. In addition to hands-on safety training programs, we have introduced interactive training software that employees can use at home.

I'm also a strong believer in variable compensation. Because we are a flat organization, we seek to acknowledge employee contributions across all functions. In line with this concept, our drivers and mechanics also receive performance bonuses. When you think about it (as I did), this practice makes so much sense. In the course of delivering and picking up equipment at construction or industrial sites, drivers probably meet more customers than any other job category in the company. Mechanics, because they service everything from excavators to air compressors, are critical to maintaining the quality of the equipment we rent. Their performance directly influences how RSC is perceived by customers and their overall experience. I'm proud and pleased that we have an inclusive program that drives the desired performance at all levels.

We recognize and reward our employees as often as we can—and this does not always have to involve monetary incentives. Recently I received an e-mail that a store had been accident-free for five years, which is a fantastic result. Based on this news, I invited the whole store to have lunch on me—a simple but appreciated small gesture. I always like to find opportunities to show our employees that I see their hard work at all levels.

Best Practices for Communicating Effectively

Best practices for communicating effectively start with taking the time to interact with your employees. I use a number of different methods to communicate and remain fully engaged across the company.

Each quarter I host a companywide, 4,200-employee conference call, during which I tell everyone how we did that quarter, what we reported to the market, and what that means for RSC, and following which I invite questions.

There may also be several opportunities throughout each quarter for ad hoc companywide communications to highlight new developments or key initiatives. These ad hoc communications add emphasis and serve to keep employees up to speed.

I also talk with many of our employees and spend time in the field. I set up a special e-mailbox, "CEO Chat," and encourage all employees to send me their concerns, issues, or whatever they want to share. I make a point to answer those e-mails when they come in. Aside from CEO Chat, I e-mail all employees quite frequently. The aforementioned Friday morning calls with the management team are effective for cascading information down into the organization. We typically have the top twenty-five to thirty leaders of the company on those calls. Once a month I also have a call with the top 150 people in the organization about the previous month's results, what we learned from them, and what we need to do in the coming month.

While none of these practices is revolutionary, they are often undervalued by leadership as effective means to reach employees. Being consistent with communication does have meaningful impact on a workforce and will lead to improved performance.

Leadership Challenges

I have experienced a range of leadership challenges and have found that there is no unsolvable problem, provided you remain focused. When I came to the equipment rental business, my manufacturing background was viewed by some as a weakness, or irrelevant. Most people in the company wondered what I knew about equipment rental and questioned how I could help an organization in flux. Consequently, I had to overcome the credibility gap that occurs when you step into a new industry. In such situations, you have to draw on your experience base and show that many things are similar and that the knowledge is transferable. As it turned out, the experience I brought from the manufacturing side has been quite helpful to our success. Applying lean, flow, and continuous improvement techniques has helped us perform more efficiently and guide our growth in the industrial sector.

Of all the different challenges I have encountered, the most difficult is adjusting the size of the company during tough times. Letting good people go is never easy. However, you must think about the employees who remain and keep the focus on doing the best thing for all stakeholders of the company. The difficulty lies in doing enough. I always coach my team to do more than they think is necessary because you almost always underestimate what needs to be done.

Importance of Speed and Agility

I talk about the importance of change and urgency all the time; we have to be able to embrace change and do so with a sense of purpose and speed. This belief has been instilled in RSC's culture. Our people are open to change, and as a result, we can maintain an organization that is flat and flexible. Flexibility means that you have to stay on top of what's going on in the present, and you have to anticipate what's coming next and take corrective action immediately. This is why I insist that we not wait around to see our numbers. We have to establish informed expectations that are based on real-time information. This is based on expectancy values, which we use to take immediate corrective action, instead of waiting for the month-end results.

Throughout my career, expectancy values have helped me and the companies I've worked for because they allow corrective actions to be taken before you have the final answer. My impatience can be a good quality (depending on how you look at it). I like to see problems being addressed or opportunities pursued as soon as possible. I need to see that people are working on issues we have identified. We can always discuss how long it will take to fix something, but I want to see that someone has started on it.

Key Takeaways

- Transparency and access foster accountability. The more information you share, the better decisions your company makes— and these decisions can be made further down in the organization if the people have the information they need.
- Coaching is a great way to spread important ideas, give recognition to people, and grow leadership within an organization.
- Best practices for effective communication start with taking the time to interact with employees at every level of your organization.
- Understand what's going on in the present, and anticipate and plan for the future. Informed expectations based on real-time information allow for immediate corrective action.

Erik Olsson has served as president, chief executive officer, and a director of RSC Holdings since 2006. He joined RSC in 2001 as chief financial officer and in 2005 became RSC's chief operating officer. RSC rents equipment and provides maintenance and support services to approximately 300,000 industrial and non-residential construction businesses across North America.

Mr. Olsson applies manufacturing models to enhance the RSC's industry-leading position and increase shareholder value. He built a business model that delivers the highest value to RSC's customers through a decentralized network of stores and on-site services. RSC's superior customer service continues to outperform the market by offering innovative products and services and surpassing customer expectations in availability, reliability, and safety. By focusing the company on high-margin rental revenues and active fleet management, Mr. Olsson is helping RSC achieve significant market share gains while sustaining attractive returns on capital employed.

Under Mr. Olsson's leadership, RSC became a public company in 2007, traded on the New York Stock Exchange (NYSE:RRR).

Prior to 2001, Mr. Olsson held a number of senior financial management positions at Atlas Copco Group in Sweden, Brazil, and the United States, including his most recent assignment as chief financial officer for Milwaukee Electric Tool Corporation in Milwaukee from 1998 to 2000.

Mr. Olsson has a degree in business administration and finance from the University of Gothenburg.

Dedication: *In memory of my dear friend, colleague, and mentor, Freek Nijdam (1941-2008).*

The Importance of Checks and Balances

David E. Scher

Chief Executive Officer

First Step Realty Inc.

ASPATORE

Introduction

I earned my real estate license while I was still in high school, and I believe getting involved in the industry at such a young age truly gave my company a competitive advantage. By the time I was twenty-three, I had five years of experience under my belt, while most others were just starting out in the brokerage business.

When I founded First Step Realty in 2004, it was very small and had only ten staff members. We recently had our five-year anniversary, and we have managed to achieve multiple goals within that timeframe. Among them is not only survival over the 90 percent of startups that fail within the first five years, but a healthy positive cash flow, as well. Additionally, First Step Realty had managed to carve its niche in the Boston bank and government (Housing and Urban Development, or HUD) foreclosure market. Achieving these and other goals was largely attributed to a sophisticated proprietary technologically driven business model (Patent US60/898,723). This intellectual property supported dozens of sales associates and affiliated contractors in-house and extending its reach to India.

One of our early challenges as a company was simply recognizing the large difference between opening a franchise and starting a company from scratch. My goal was to build something that was unique, creative, and personal. I believe First Step Realty embodies these aspects. In contrast, when you open a franchise, you must face corporate support, oversight, legacy systems, and other corporate requirements. Furthermore, the corporation provides a training manual to help guide the franchise in its business, which is especially true for real estate brokerages. When we created First Step in 2004, there was no training manual. Everything had to be built from the ground up.

After the attacks on 9/11, I remember discussing the effects of inflation on the real estate market and how it was a temporary solution to offset the economic shock that occurred from the terrorist attacks. When I founded First Step, I focused the company in the direction of bank and government foreclosures immediately. It is a niche market, and there are only four other authorized brokers in Boston. With very slight exception, we have handled every listing from the HUD in the past three years.

Managing the Budget

When the company opened, we did not have conventional investors, so we needed to be creative to manage our money efficiently. When we needed to create our proprietary system, for instance, we negotiated with a small information technology (IT) startup filled with talented people. We agreed to provide them with office space and the resources to get started, and in exchange, they would provide us with their IT services. An added benefit of this agreement is that since the IT company shares our location, whenever a problem arises or we want to make a change, it can occur immediately.

Our proprietary system has made all the difference in our gaining a competitive edge in the real estate industry. In fact, in 2007 we had a patent in the trademark office for the system. Our real estate brokerage system is not just a database; it is a business model we have used to capture the entire business of brokerage, which must account for any number of variables. No two transactions are exactly alike, so the industry is quite difficult to systemize, but we have managed it fairly successfully. Our system is self-propelling and has checks and balances.

Another way we have saved money is through our internship program for college students. It is an unpaid opportunity, but in exchange, our interns receive college credits and industry experience. If they are successful and show potential, we offer them paid positions upon completion of the internship.

Accountability Is Key

Accountability is one of the most important values that need to be stressed in any organization, but especially so in brokerage, so this is an important aspect of my leadership approach. We place a huge emphasis on comprehensive and thorough training and verification, so everyone needs to be accountable. Without accountability, the entire corporate process and business would likely collapse. For example, we hold associates accountable for their initial training process, and we test them on it. After the associate passes the training exams, he or she cannot later shift the burden onto mistakes or errors he or she was previously trained and tested on.

Every link in the chain of command has to hold the link above and the link below accountable for its actions. If I focus on our values, mission, and vision, then the office managers can feel free to focus on internal office policies, and the branch sales managers can focus on the performance of their respective associates, while the associates focus on their core competency: sales. Communication is an essential part of achieving accountability. When I give an instruction, I often ask the person to paraphrase those instructions back to me to verify that he or she understood what I said and provide them with the opportunity to ask questions.

Changes in the Industry

The real estate industry itself has also changed dramatically in the last decade. Previously, listings were written by hand in a book, but now everything is computerized. At one time, you had to go through a broker to gain access to listings; whereas, now, 85 percent of home buyers conduct their own online research using multiple channels before ever meeting with a Realtor.

Given all these changes, I have learned one important lesson: I am not in the business of selling real estate. Rather, I am in the business of creating an attractive setting and hiring, retaining, and creating successful sales associates. These associates are the business; they act as independent contractors, and they bring in all the revenue. Their entire salary is based on commission, and my entire business is based on their bringing in revenue for the company. Consequently, I have to make them comfortable and happy as employees and train them as quickly as possible to provide them with the tools they need to do their best to earn money for both themselves and the business.

Early in the business, managers handled all that training, which was a time-consuming process that took up all their available time. Now, however, we have a more systematic approach. For example, our largest training sections consist of Office Policy, Procedure, and Resources. Once the associate has been exposed to and has reviewed the material, he or she must pass a written test on it before moving on to the next training section, such as the

Hands-on Sales and the field training portion, where he or she must now pass a one-on-one oral exam administered by a member of management.

The training for a new associate with no experience is different from the training for an associate who has already worked in the business. Specifically, much of the initial training focuses on office policies, procedures, resources, how to use our resources, and how to handle various aspects of the business. New associates receive this training before going out into the field and representing our brand name. New associates with veteran field experience do not require the same degree of hands-on sales training.

We take this training very seriously, and until they complete it, associates are considered on probation and are not officially affiliated with our company. Even though there is no out-of-pocket expense for taking on new associates—because they work solely on commission—one hiring mistake can set a cataclysmic series of events that can destroy relationships, diminish the brand, and create a domino effect that would be very expensive to repair.

Developing Necessary Skill Sets

Agility is invaluable for our organization. Being able to adapt to different circumstances in the brokerage business is key, and in this business, there are no "right" answers. For example, there are only so many cell phones and plans to sell. While they may come together in different ways, there are truly a limited number of unique transactions you can make because you are dealing with a standardized product.

In the brokerage industry, on the other hand, every transaction is unique; no two real estate transactions are exactly alike; and more often than not, the answer will be "it depends." This leads directly into another crucial and required skill, which is problem-solving. When there are no right answers, and the questions change constantly, the ability to make a sale is often predicted by the ability to solve whatever problems have arisen. Circumstances change, and a good broker is always able to change right along with them to meet the needs of the client while still maintaining checks and balances.

A necessary part of checks and balances is making sure there are consequences for non-compliance. We have a three-strike system that helps keep associates and staff members accountable. The first strike is a warning. The associate receives an e-mail that provides indemnity for disciplining staff and reinforcing that further problems will lead to certain consequences. It is nothing more than a written warning that goes on record. The second strike is a sit-down meeting with management. Often, if the infraction is serious enough, the associate has to meet with me personally. The third strike results in termination.

It was difficult to learn to stick to this system and not take into account the personal aspects, especially since associates work on commission, so there are no direct costs to keep someone on staff. The indirect or intangible costs, however, can be significant. For example, if we were to keep an associate who did not meet certain standards, and that associate was later to make a mistake or misrepresentation to a client, legal and regulatory repercussions may often result. Since the associate is working under the scope of the organization's corporate broker's license, the company is responsible and must answer. In this scenario, most often attorneys may need to be involved. Legal representation can be costly. We learned it is best to hold everyone to the same standard, or problems spread like a virus throughout the company.

Leadership Strategies and Challenges

As chief executive officer (CEO), my role at First Step Realty has shifted over time. My initial role was mostly operational when we started: day-to-day operations, hiring, firing, and recruiting. Now I have moved into more of a leadership position. I believe you have to lead by example, and people need to see behavior modeled multiple times before they can successfully emulate it. Sometimes it is helpful for a new associate to experience a short-term failure or rejection to gauge how they will react to it. Failure is naturally a part of this industry—not every phone call will lead to a sale.

Additionally, my age was a definite obstacle when I started this company. Many of the affiliated associates and staff members were my age or older; yet I was the boss, and it certainly was a challenge. When the firm First Step Realty was founded, at the time, like many twenty-two-year-olds, I felt the need to constantly prove myself when the staff questioned my experience and my knowledge. More often than not, a new business is highly reflective of its founders or owners. Over time, after much trial and error, I implemented a more effective approach and began emphasizing more accountability of sales associates and staff. Now, company personnel are held accountable for their performance and actions, accordingly rather than proving how acting differently may have been a better approach. As the company has aged itself and become successful, the topic of my age rarely enters into a discussion.

In the future, I hope to lead our organization to branch out as a national franchise, using our unique technologically driven business model to gain a competitive edge in various markets.

Key Takeaways

- Know your industry. By looking ahead, you can place your organization into the perfect niche and make a name for yourself in the market.

- Save money whenever possible. Partner with other companies to share services; find ways to scout talent; and build what you can from scratch when necessary. It may be harder in the short term, but it will give you a competitive advantage in the long term if you can distinguish building something that will be valuable and unique versus re-creating the wheel.

- When training is complete, don't just give people a test—make them show how they can use what they have learned in the field. There is no better way to learn than through hands-on experience.

- Everyone should be accountable for his or her own actions and behaviors, and if they fail to meet the standards of the company, the consequences should be swift and even.

David E. Scher's accomplishments as a successful broker and chief executive officer of First Step Realty Inc. include being the #1 seller of Housing and Urban Development (HUD) foreclosures in the Boston area (one of seven who specialize in this sector of the local real estate market). This level of productivity has been attained by the combined implementation of a (US898,723, patent pending) state-of-the-art Internet-based marketing strategy, which goes well beyond the limited conventional advertising tools, such as using only the Multiple Listing System (MLS) to market government and bank foreclosure properties. To help clients market homes in the overlapping New England markets, Mr. Scher uses a customized system to feed MLS listings from four states.

Current brokerage operations demand innovative thinking and execution strategies, along with a knowledgeable team, guaranteeing the property cycle from listing to closing will proceed seamlessly in the shortest time possible. As part of being a full-service provider to the real estate-owned (REO), HUD, and foreclosure industry Mr. Scher, an e-Pro Certified Realtor and HUD Authorized Broker, has a qualified team of property preservation professionals capable of completing all necessary tasks and functions required to close the sale.

Mr. Scher leverages his brokerage with an in-house information technology (IT) company. Having a team of specialized computer programmers ensures a competitive advantage by leveraging continuous innovation of database systems and processes that further simplify the conventional real estate transaction, thereby making his firm more attractive to buyers, sellers, and salespersons.

Earning his real estate license at age eighteen, Mr. Scher worked his way through college at four different companies before opening his own brokerage in June 2004. He was featured in the June 2006 cover article, "30 Under 30," in Realtor *magazine, published by The National Association of Realtors.*

Acknowledgment: *Brenna Barr, First Step Realty and Gary Jennison, Corcoran-Jennison.*

Recognizing Leadership Opportunities in Unlikely Places

Mike Thompson

President and Chief Executive Officer

Groupware Technology Inc.

ASPATORE

The Essence of the CEO Position: Leading by Example

Groupware Technology specializes in the design, procurement, testing, and integration of information technology (IT) solutions. Supported by a relentless dedication to service, we are technology experts focused on solving strategic business problems and providing insight and leadership to our customers and the industry.

In my role as president and chief executive officer (CEO) of Groupware Technology, I am tasked with setting the vision for the company—who we want to be and what we need to do to be successful in the marketplace. This includes developing and communicating our objectives, coupled with a set of clear, attainable, and measurable goals, and setting the standards by which we operate. I've learned these responsibilities are a constant; in other words, because the front line is focused on the day-to-day operations, a CEO cannot just lay out the vision, objectives, goals, and standards and expect the team to follow suit. The CEO has to live them and be a constant reminder of why these are important to the company. The essence of this role is to lead by example.

Another important responsibility is creating an environment where there is not only the opportunity for immediate success, but also one in which consistent success becomes the standard. The common term used is "corporate culture," but I see it as more than this. Having been in the corporate structure of the technical industry for the better part of my career, I have observed the failings of a corporate culture conceived and developed by management and then mandated to the front line. Individuals respond much more positively when they can contribute to the process of developing the culture. For example, when determining the company's values, I sought input from our team. Together, we established Groupware's values of customer service, excellence, fun, and giving back.

Being the Face of the Company

As president and CEO of the company, the greatest evolution has been coming to the true understanding that I am *the face of the company*. As such, one of the understated responsibilities in leading a company is understanding how you are perceived by the industry at large, your peers, and your team.

Regardless of what kind of day I'm having, I am fully aware of how my actions can and do affect the energy in the office. My day-to-day attitude is on constant display, and I am keenly aware of my effect on the rest of the team. The successes we have experienced have allowed the company to participate in more lucrative opportunities. However, being recognized as an industry expert and a thought leader comes with a price—time.

I travel often, spending time with customers, vendors, and manufacturers. But when I return to the office, I make it a point to visit with the team, ask them how things are progressing, and, when needed, roll up my sleeves and jump in on whatever task is at hand. Two of the most difficult things to learn are trust and patience—trusting the team to perform the tasks, and patience while allowing them to learn at their pace. These two aspects are important because once the individuals have internalized the problem-solving process, they will deliver greater results and greater returns, both in profitability and in customer satisfaction.

Business Growth and the Evolution of Individual Roles

As the business has grown, my responsibilities and obligations have, naturally, also evolved. The demand for my time is now stretched with running the business and sitting on several industry advisory councils and community boards. The balance here is to remain true to the purpose of the councils, genuinely contribute on their behalf, and avoid the mindset of mining opportunities for your company.

To attract and retain the best and the brightest, especially in the highly competitive industry of technology, you need to deliver on both the perceived and the promised benefits. Having benefited from the rigors of a higher education myself, I found when one is building a strong team, one should encourage the further education and training of all who wish to elevate their careers. An example of this is the recent completion of an executive business degree by our vice president of operations. Our program reimburses team members who complete their designated educational goals.

Also, all of the studies we have seen indicate those in management who can improve their presentation skills stand a better chance of advancing their careers. To this end, we contracted a professional speaker coach who uses relevant, real-world business topics as part of the coaching. Because our business is on a highly technical level, our engineers often accompany our sales team. We've found this approach delivers more closed sales opportunities. We have now included several of our top engineers in the speaker coaching program with positive results. Again, the employee is given the opportunity to enhance the breadth of their experiences. My personal belief is simple: a company cannot grow if the leadership team does not grow as individuals. It is my responsibility to mentor and motivate their growth and to continue to challenge myself to grow, as well.

Taking Care of the Team

Like many other companies, we offer our team quarterly bonuses for achieving specific goals. But, as previously mentioned, fun is one of our core values, and this goes beyond the requisite fun at company gatherings.

All employees get to participate in and benefit from the success of the company. They do so by achieving set goals. Benefits include an annual trip to a desired resort location, which, when coupled with other goals, allows them the opportunity to also bring their families. The health of our team is important to the health of our company and ultimately our success. To this end, we provide an aggressive benefits plan, which includes a comprehensive health plan, a 401(k) plan, a 401(k) matching and profit-sharing plan, and gym membership reimbursement.

The Power of Listening

Clear communication is the cornerstone of any successful organization, and I, along with senior management, promote an open-door policy to all. The time spent listening to our team always produces positive—and at times even innovative—results.

Along with an open-door policy, we've structured the organization to facilitate opportunities for all to actively engage in determining the direction of the company. We accomplish this through weekly manager meetings, having senior management walk the halls actively asking questions, and engaging fully in the exchange of ideas, concerns, and suggestions brought forth by team members. As a company, we assemble for an annual business meeting over a two-day period, where the objectives and goals are delivered to all at the same time. We then follow up on the status of the stated objectives and goals at our quarterly all-hands meetings.

Since we have offices in several locations around the western United States, as well as sales personnel out in the field, we have invested in video conferencing for the regional offices and those in the field. This allows everyone the opportunity to be briefed on the company's status in real time. We've found this to be instrumental in particular for the field personnel because they can use the most current information when dealing with their customers, which, again, can lead to closing a sale or responding to a concern.

The Power of Giving

Of the four core values at Groupware, we are proudest of the value of giving back. Being a member of the Campbell, California, business community affords us a safe and friendly environment in which to conduct our business. In my personal life, I've always believed charity starts at home; I believe it holds true in business life, as well. Over the years, we've raised funds for organizations in the Campbell community that care for those less fortunate. Some of the activities we've been involved with include fund-raising events, monetary contributions, and gathering team members to volunteer their most precious asset—time. Because we are in the technology business, we have donated computer products on several occasions to help organizations become more efficient, and the donations allow them to apply more of the funds to their cause, rather than to the operation of the charity.

Regarding our commitment to the environment, I recognize being conscientious of not only our global environment, but also our immediate environment, is a reflection of our values. So I initiated a goal to become a "green company," which we achieved in 2008 and for which we were recognized by the county of Santa Clara, California. Some may see this as self-serving and perhaps a nice public relations feather in our cap, but I believe it's having a positive impact on the team and all those who enter our corporate offices.

In recent years the business world has been slowly awakening to the advantages of being environmentally friendly. The rising costs of maintaining the basic business operations have led to the development of green data centers, which are major consumers of power and generators of heat. Having experienced the "sticker shock" of our power bill, I began converting our data center into a greener data center. And although the initial investment seemed high, the long-term financial benefits more than justified the expense. Not only did we reduce our overall energy bill, but we also began offering sustainability solutions through architecting future data centers and transforming them into green data centers. We now have the capability to demonstrate an actual return on investment to our end-users, not only financially for them, but also for their environments. These actions clearly illustrate "the power is in the giving."

Executing at the Moment of Truth

During my time as an executive vice president, the technology industry had a period in its history many would like to forget: the "dot-com implosion," "dot-bomb," "www.what were we thinking?" The Internet hit the business world with a force, and suddenly everyone rushed to own an e-commerce business. Millions of dollars changed hands; hip new offices sprung up where none had existed; and the promise of a new industry intoxicated the Silicon Valley and beyond. Then it all came crashing down like a house of cards, and no one escaped the wreck, including me. My employer at the time charged me with managing a severe reduction in force, which included many employees with whom I had built relationships. Balancing my professional obligations with my personal feelings proved to be a major challenge, but I managed through and carried the lessons learned with me into my present position.

Just when you think you've been through the worst, something invariably surfaces. The recent bubble-burst, which sent the economy into a tailspin, looked to be daunting indeed. However, what I learned from my previous endeavors prepared me to handle the crisis. I knew the best way to prepare for any possible threat to the company's future would be to gather a strong team who had been through similar experiences and who understood the importance of staying focused on the customer. Rather than enacting financial cutbacks, we invested in a proof-of-concept lab, honed our operation expenditures, hired more team members to strengthen our bench, and offered more services. Though we had lower revenue on the front end of the crisis, we never lost a customer and, in fact, gained market share. I call this executing at the moment of truth.

The Question and Quest for Innovation

I've always found the question of being innovative peculiar and, at times, even funny because it's not as if one has the time to just sit around and think of ways to be innovative. For me, innovation happens while in the process of working on a solution to an issue. Once I find a viable solution, it seems to take on the perception of an innovation.

For example, a few years ago, I began to take note of the industry evolution from the customer's point of view to the manufacturer's. After I shared my ideas with senior management, the team decided to build out a first-class data center coupled with a proof-of-concept lab. This would allow customers the opportunity to come to the lab and test the solution our engineers designed. The strategic advantage for the customer is in letting them have the experience of running the solution before making the investment. Now, in and of itself, this is certainly not an earth-shattering innovation, but it is a practical one, which is in keeping with our core value of customer service excellence. A side benefit from this innovation came from the manufacturers, who now want to bring their latest technology into the lab for our customers to experience.

From a branding standpoint, the Groupware Technology lab is now known as the place to visit if you want to gain familiarity with the most up-to-date technology. I once read that when a scientist actually discovers something or comes upon some revolutionary breakthrough, *"Eureka, I've found it!"* is not exactly the reaction. It actually falls more along the lines of, *"Huh, that's funny."* I believe this to be the case with many innovations and discoveries.

Advice for Other Leaders of Today and Tomorrow

The most important lesson I've learned throughout my business career is you can never know it all, and you certainly don't have the time to invest in trying. Otherwise, you'll spend your life learning and never executing. And executing is where action delivers results.

As for advice I would share with others, I'd have to share the advice of the many other successful leaders who came before me, from a myriad of backgrounds—develop an excellent plan with a clear objective and achievable goals, and then surround yourself with a highly talented team and let them execute the plan.

In today's business world and in the foreseeable future, there are and will be hundreds of books to guide you through your career, offering "*the*" steps to success or "*the*" habits of the successful. I've found they can serve as a guide, but are by no means a definitive blueprint. As a leader, you are the decision-maker. You can give your best effort in the process, but one never truly knows whether any decision is the correct one until the impact of the decision is known. To this I can add only, make a decision based on the best information available, but by all means, make the decision. Your team is waiting for your leadership. Finally—and I learned this well into my position as president and CEO of Groupware Technology—identify your company's core values, communicate them repeatedly to the team at every opportunity, and then live them.

As president and chief executive officer of Groupware Technology Inc., Mike Thompson provides the leadership and vision essential for propelling companywide success. His cross-functional skill set, innate business savvy, and real-world understanding enable him to provide the creativity and strategy needed to build and grow a successful organization.

With more than a decade of industry experience, Mr. Thompson spends much of his time managing all phases of the business process. Starting from the ground up, he has gained extensive experience and an overall respect for all organizational platforms.

Responsible for setting the vision, developing the strategy, and managing the execution of corporate initiatives and goals, Mr. Thompson is actively involved in managing and developing relationships and strategic alliances with vendors, partners, and end-users. He has been recognized for his work in improving operational efficiencies to enhance the end-user experience and overall satisfaction, and has proved his ability to increase profitable revenues year over year.

Recognized by the industry for his thought leadership, Mr. Thompson sits on several advisory boards. He is also active in helping fellow entrepreneurs who are interested in his expertise and experience. He has built the foundation for Groupware to continue its unprecedented growth and success.

Mr. Thompson earned a Bachelor of Science degree from the University of Southern California and an MBA, graduating with honors, from Regis University.

Redefining Success

Julia Klein
Chair and Chief Executive Officer
C.H. Briggs Company

ASPATORE

Evolving Roles

I am the chair, chief executive officer (CEO), and majority stockholder of C.H. Briggs Company, one of the nation's largest independently owned distributors of specialty building materials. Our company, started by my grandparents more than forty years ago, has undergone many changes in the twenty years since I took over. In my role as CEO, I am focused on strategy, growth, and culture, and our president and chief operating officer (COO) runs the operations of the business, supported by a strong leadership team.

It can be easy to become mired in the details of operating a business, so the move from owner/operator to owner/strategist was, for me, deliberately in response to the needs of the business. A business needs to be professionally managed, and it cannot become too dependent on any one person. Such a dependency is not good for the culture, for growth, or for eventual exit. My choice to move into new roles necessitated stepping back, which has resulted in greater growth for everyone else. Our approach is different from the one taken by many mid-market, closely held companies.

My changing role in the company has come with certain challenges, but the important ingredient in reaching the decision to change has been self-awareness. My new role is a better fit for my skills and interests. After twenty years of running the business, I had some history with the company, and there were areas where I was deeply attached. Our president and COO —whose leadership is excellent—and I have talked through all these changes. He is comfortable with consulting me as needed, and I have learned to hold back at times when my experience or advice has not been sought. Once I determined that it was best for the company to have someone else running the operation, I was able to let another person take that role.

Leadership Style

I have an open, independent style of leadership, and I believe strongly in open communication. We have changed the culture of this business over two decades because when open communication is embraced by only one person at the top, it is not terribly effective. Part of my challenge has been creating a team that shares our values and can express them to the whole company. We started as a family business, but today we are a business family. As a company, we are professionally managed with strong family values and a strong family heritage. It is important that we find ways to give back to the community, that we have ample opportunities for professional development, and that we are of service to our customers, our vendors, and each other.

As in many midmarket, family-owned companies, we have experienced a generational shift. My grandparents founded the company in their garage— a true, all-American entrepreneurial success story—and as time went on, my father took over the company. His style was dynamic and entrepreneurial, a maverick kind of leadership. During the 1970s and 1980s, his style was the prevalent style in most entrepreneurial companies in the country, directive and top-down, and it was successful for a long time.

When I came into the company in 1989, my father told me a story about how fabulous the view is when you are sitting on top of a pointed pyramid, looking down, but that while it is a great view, it gets to be uncomfortable over the years. I realized that I did not have the same personality, and it was a different time; sitting at the point of a pyramid would not work for me or our company going forward. I thought of the image of flipping that pyramid, where my job was to support the team that supported all of the people in the company that supported our customers and our vendors, with the point of the pyramid being at the bottom, and I think that image has worked well in changing the culture of the company to match changing times. Over twenty years, we have also had many staff changes, and I have been able to recruit an excellent group of leaders who have helped grow the company and then see it through the downturn in the economy in the past couple of years.

Relationships with C-Level Executives

I have recruited, hired, or promoted all the C-level executives presently serving our company, and over time, I have put together a group of intelligent, experienced thinkers, operators, and leaders. As a group, they have disparate personalities; they are different from me, and they are different from one another, which I believe makes for the best decision-

and strategy-making, although it is not always the easiest way to run a business. Sometimes it is easier to have people who completely agree with you and with each other, but that approach is smoother—not necessarily better. When I realized how much of a challenge it was to knit together a group of people who are so smart and have such disparate approaches, I realized I needed a president who excels in team-building and managing these group dynamics. Finding that person has taken the team to a whole different level.

From my perspective as chair and CEO, I watch and ask questions to ensure that the strategy is on target and that we are meeting our milestones. I do not meet on a daily basis with individual leaders, but I do meet regularly with the president to work on our whole strategic planning process and issues involved with strategy, such as ensuring that we are making the right investments in human capital and that people are developing in the ways we have identified. I communicate through town meetings with the entire company every quarter, and I meet with the leadership team as they need me. I help set the stage, and the president directs the show.

Developing Co-Workers

One of the primary ingredients in co-worker development—and I include myself in this—is continuous learning. I have always gained from extensive reading, and I profit from peer and professional groups, as well, which have allowed me to sound out ideas and new approaches with people in different industries.

I try to model the kind of continuous learning and self-development I want my co-workers to use. All of the C-level executives, as part of our strategic planning process, build in team development, team building, and professional development so that people are setting their own personal and professional goals right along with our main objectives for the next year or two. That is an approach our president brought to us; we now view personal and professional development in concert. At first I was skeptical —how did buying new software and losing twenty pounds fit together?— but I realized that when you are trying to create the world, the business, and the life you want, you do a gap analysis, and then you set yourself the task of reducing the gap. It is the same process, both personally and professionally, and it has worked well.

Therefore, we have a management team of about thirty who meet monthly to discuss operational issues, share experiences, and find ways to better communicate with one another. We often bring in an outside speaker, such as customers addressing the group about the changing nature of their businesses and our bankers talking about the changing credit and equity markets so our people can see how the decisions they make on what inventory to purchase directly affect how the bank views us.

We have also recently hired a leadership team member to focus solely on human capital. For as much as we have talked about human resources and have conducted extensive one-on-one coaching, our actual investment has not matched our rhetoric. This investment has taken much of the coaching, development, and teaching away from the president and away from me, freeing our resources. For myself, I have always made use of executive coaching. We contract with an executive coach to work with the leadership team and with me, as needed, and I've really benefited from my peer groups in TEC/Vistage, Committee of 200, and Young Presidents' Organization.

Leadership Challenges

Because we are in the construction industry, the economy's recent nosedive hit us hard and has presented challenges on several levels. First, we lost nearly 25 percent of our top line almost overnight, so operationally and physically, we had to figure out how to manage that loss. Next, we had our first layoff in the history of the business, which was difficult and sad, and then we faced rethinking all of our operations so that we could continue to survive and be profitable in a different environment.

One type of challenge has been helping people redefine success in a different era. We had eighteen years of tremendous growth and eighteen months of falling off a cliff; that is a short period to redefine what it means to be successful today. Many of our competitors are no longer in business, so surviving is success, but we had been accustomed to something more than survival. Redefining success has generated a great deal of conversation and planning for the future, now that we have made it through that difficult era.

Our agility has been a key piece in being able to change, and then change again, and then change again. We have to not only react but also try to stay ahead. Being comfortable with ambiguity is as important as being agile and quick because there is not much that is truly black and white, especially today. The business climate is murky, with little visibility. Even when business was on an upswing, it was not always black and white. People issues are complex, and customer issues are complex; sometimes not having perfect answers gives you time to think and plan, which also makes you purposely hear more sides of the story. You get better decision-making that way, which is a critical skill both personally and organizationally.

Accountability

In an ideal world, we are clear about what we want to get done, and then it gets done. In reality, it never works quite so perfectly. Therefore, accountability is paramount in ensuring that duties, tasks, and responsibilities are executed as needed.

Having that accountability has been, for us, twofold. First, we hire people who are self-motivated. Self-motivated people have accountability built in, and they provide a model for others to follow. Second, the president of our company knows how to drive accountability in a low-key and kind way. We have adopted an approach taken from *Mastering the Rockefeller Habits* by Verne Harnish, who is a thinker and leader in the small-business world. His approach builds in accountability through the technique of constant communication.

In our company, we have daily huddles throughout the leadership team every morning, where we review how we did yesterday, what is up for today, and what obstacles are in the way. Every person addresses those areas as they relate to that person's responsibilities and commitments, which reinforces accountability within the group.

From there, the huddle effect trickles down so that everybody in the business meets with their teams in quick, ten-minute meetings, addressing the same areas. We also have good leaders who check in with their people and get them to internalize accountability.

Concluding Advice

I began this chapter discussing emotional intelligence, so it is fitting to conclude with a discussion about how emotional intelligence can affect a business.

Hiring the right people is the epitome of knowing yourself. You know what you can do and what you are good at; by hiring people who can take care of other aspects of business, you are free to do the things that only you can do, that you are good at, and that you will enjoy doing. When you spend too much time working on things you're not very good at, you don't do them well, and you impede everyone else along the way.

Key Takeaways

- A business needs to be professionally managed, but it cannot become too dependent on any one person. Such a dependency is not good for the culture; it is not good for growth; and it is not good for eventual exit.
- It is important to find ways to give back to the community, to have ample opportunities for professional development, and to be of service to customers, to vendors, and to each other.
- The view is fabulous when you are sitting on top of a pointed pyramid, looking down. It is a great view, but sitting on the point gets to be uncomfortable and ineffective over the years.
- Being comfortable with ambiguity is as important as being smart because there is not much that is truly black and white, especially today.
- Sometimes not having perfect answers gives you time to think and plan and makes you purposely hear more sides of the story. You get better decision-making that way, which is a critical skill both personally and organizationally.

Julia Klein, owner, chairwoman, and chief executive officer, has led the transformation of C.H. Briggs Company from family business to growth platform company, expanding its products, geography, and markets; introducing innovative technology; and integrating two acquisitions.

Now one of the nation's top 100 women-owned businesses, the company has experienced dramatic growth during Ms. Klein's tenure, and has been in the top quartile for profitability in its industry segment for eighteen years.

Ms. Klein developed the company from hardware distributor into distributor of a wide range of building materials, known for its early and innovative application of technology. Under her leadership, C.H. Briggs became the first company in its industry segment to deliver full service online, and the first to offer a green building product line. When C.H. Briggs introduced its green product line in 2004, it dedicated two Leadership in Energy and Environmental Design (LEED)-certified coworkers to the job of educating customers on what it means to supply a LEED-certified building. This approach to doing business has earned the company the Most Innovative Supplier Support Program award presented by Kitchen & Bath Design News.

Today, C.H. Briggs is an organization of 170 coworkers, with more than 200 vendors and 15,000 customers in Pennsylvania, New Jersey, Delaware, Maryland, the District of Columbia, Virginia, North Carolina, South Carolina, Georgia, Eastern Tennessee, Ohio, Indiana, and Michigan.

The company was twice named a national winner in the Inc. magazine/Cisco Systems Growing with Technology awards. Ms. Klein was invited by the National Association of Wholesaler-Distributors to speak on the live satellite broadcast, "Success on the Internet—Real World Strategies for Wholesalers-Distributors," which also featured C.H. Briggs as a case study.

The National Association of Wholesaler-Distributors invited Ms. Klein to participate in the live Webcast, "Surviving 2002—Real World Strategies for Wholesalers-Distributors," with President George W. Bush. She also traveled to Northern Ireland with the U.S. Department of State to encourage Internet business among Irish entrepreneurs.

Ms. Klein is a former board member of the National Association of Wholesaler-Distributors Research and Education Foundation, a founding member of the Cabinet Industry Distribution Association, and a former board member of the North American Building Materials Distribution Association. She also serves on the Corporate Advisory Board of Modern Distribution Management magazine.

Serving on the Advisory Board of Quaker Maid Meats Inc. and Arbill Safety Supply Company, Ms. Klein is also a member of the Young Presidents' Organization and the Committee of 200, an international organization of women who own and run companies and who lead corporations as top executives and board members.

Ms. Klein was named a finalist in the Ernst & Young 2008 Entrepreneur Of The Year® awards for Greater Philadelphia. She has been honored among Pennsylvania's 50 Best Women in Business. The Women's Business Enterprise Council awarded her the Women Who Are Changing America award in 2005.

Ms. Klein is on the Advisory Board of the Reading Hospital and Medical Center and a member of many hospital committees. She has been honored as Distinguished Girl Scout Alumna for her leadership development of local young women by Girl Scouts of Eastern Pennsylvania and received the Community Service Award from Caron Treatment Centers. Ms. Klein received the 2004 ATHENA Award, a national program that promotes women's leadership and honors an individual for her business accomplishments and community service. She was also honored as Junior Achievement Hall of Fame award winner in 2008 for her commitment to the community and young people.

Known for its contributions to the community, C.H. Briggs has received the Corporate Citizenship Award, Employee Campaign Award and Eagle Award from Berks County United Way. It also earned a national Community Service Award from Kitchen & Bath Design News.

Following graduate school, Ms. Klein ran political campaigns for state, congressional, and presidential races through four campaign cycles. Because each political contest is a startup, Ms. Klein believes experience in the political arena is good training for an entrepreneur. Her passion for building a business, creating jobs, and influencing communities came out of politics and gave her a chance, early in her career, to exercise strategic and quick thinking.

Ms. Klein joined C.H. Briggs in 1989 as general manager of a newly opened branch in Baltimore. She purchased the business in 1991, and in 1994 moved to the company's headquarters in Reading, Pennsylvania, becoming president and chief executive officer, and chairwoman in 2007 after hiring Donald F. Schalk as president and chief operating officer.

Ms. Klein's commitment to enhancing opportunities in the world of commerce for women business owners led C.H. Briggs to become WBENC (Women's Business Enterprise National Council)-certified. The company has been named one of the top ten Women's Business Enterprises by the Women's Business Development Center.

C.H. Briggs is regularly recognized among the top women-owned businesses in the nation by Women's Enterprise USA *magazine,* Working Woman *magazine and* Enterprising Women *magazine.*

After graduating from the College of Wooster with a B.A, Ms. Klein went on to earn an MA in public policy from the University of Chicago, where she was an Urban Scholars Fellow.

Ms. Klein is married to Eric Jenkins, and they have a teenage son.

Leading a Spin-Off Business through Change

Randall D. Stilley
President and Chief Executive Officer
Seahawk Drilling Inc.

ASPATORE

Introduction

As chief executive officer (CEO) of Seahawk, a spin-off of Pride International, I am also the founder, the strategist, and the one who put together the management team and recruited the board of directors. Until recently, my responsibilities were focused on trying to build a business management team that would allow us to operate as a separate public company. Since August 2009, much of what I have done involves implementing our initial strategies and addressing a number of crises that developed shortly after the spin-off.

Seahawk Drilling is currently the only spin-off company in our industry. Because we are also the newest company in the field, my responsibilities as CEO are different from those of most of my peers, as I am not running a company with a long history or track record. This poses many challenges, such as putting together a team of people who need to operate more independently than most had been accustomed to doing. Consequently, approximately half of the employees here came from Pride International, and about half were recruited from the outside to fill in gaps we had in skill sets and in our senior management team. As a new company that is still evolving, our culture certainly creates some unique challenges, but there is also a great opportunity to build an organization that can thrive and grow in the future.

CEO Leadership Style

My role now is different from what I have done in the past as CEO at other companies. Essentially, Seahawk is similar to a startup company. I spend more time coaching and mentoring the management team, working with the board of directors, and working with the investment community than I might normally because we are trying to get our message out and convey exactly what we are about.

Consequently, I also spend a little less time with customers than I would normally. Over the next few years, my role will likely evolve into more of a traditional CEO role, where I will spend more time with customers and the investment community, and less time on internal management.

My leadership style is normally collaborative. I like to be collaborative not only with the management team, but with all of our stakeholders, as well, particularly when it involves important decisions. Over the past year, a number of crises have developed, and we do not always have time to gather all of the information we would like, so I have had to revert more to a command-and-control style of leadership on occasion to address these early challenges. A collaborative approach is typically better because it gets everybody on board, and everyone understands what is taking place in the business. However, there are times when unexpected things happen and I must step in and make quick decisions. I have learned over the years that I need to adjust my management style to effectively address certain situations.

I also solicit and appreciate feedback on my performance as CEO. Most of the feedback comes from either the board of directors or the management team. The board does an annual assessment of my performance, and I coordinate an annual assessment that my senior managers do on me, as well. I also try to get feedback from investors, and I encourage our employees to tell me what they think. It is not always easy to get employees to tell the CEO what they think of his job, but I encourage open communication, and if people have questions, I encourage them to ask.

Many times the questions people ask will give an indication of what kind of job they think I am doing. The feedback I collect is useful in refining my leadership practices. I do not work in the same manner I did twenty years ago, and I have learned to be both adaptable and flexible. Being adaptable and flexible, constantly trying to do a better job, and always seeking feedback on what I do have had a big impact on the success of my career.

One of my greatest leadership challenges was in the mid 1990s, when I moved to Malaysia as head of the Far East region for Halliburton. We had a business unit that had been losing money for several years; revenues were down, and there was no clear reason it was happening. This was a new environment for me because the business units I had worked in previously had always been successful.

I chose to look at three key areas to figure out what we could do—people, our strategy, and our customers. I quickly realized that we had too many expatriates working in the Far East, and there had not been enough effort put into developing local talent in the region. I decided to change out most of the senior management team so that more capable, talented local employees were in key positions. The expatriates that remained in the region were required to develop a training and development plan so that they would have a replacement for their job within two years. I think that helped change the entire culture in the region.

We changed our strategy at the same time, realizing that we could not be all things to all people. We started focusing on individual customers and projects, and we developed a much closer relationship with our customers in China because that was a big underutilized market. Over a period of about two years, we went from being a money loser to one of the most profitable regions in the company. Our success was geared in people, strategy, customers, and getting local employees involved in making the company successful. I've found that being adaptable is a major success factor. I try to keep this in mind: there are always new ways to do things.

Strategizing and Planning as an Agile Organization

For business planning, we set annual goals and business plans based on our strategy, and we do scenario planning because our business can be quite volatile and unpredictable. For example, because our main customer in Mexico is a national oil company that had budget difficulties, we had to move all our rigs out of the country earlier this year, which changed many things. We also had the BP oil spill in the Gulf of Mexico, which had a huge impact on every company that drills offshore in the Gulf of Mexico. Those two events forced us to change our strategy and plans in mid-stream. Even though we had used scenario planning, we did not predict a blowout and spill of this magnitude in the Gulf of Mexico, and nobody else did, either. However, our scenario planning in conjunction with our plans and goals and in thinking longer term give us a good sense of what levers we need to pull when things change. Also, we normally try to make changes and adjustments to our strategies annually, but lately we have moved to quarterly updates because of a rapidly shifting business landscape.

We try to involve people at all levels of the organization in developing our business plans; we communicate with our employees and make sure they are developing their own action plans in concert with our overall plans and goals. Because we are a young company, we do not have much opportunity to develop people internally for new positions yet. Instead, we have had to spend more time recruiting people from outside the company to fill jobs when they become available.

Normally, I like to have plans in place for management succession so that we can develop people over a period of years and then move them into the higher-level jobs; we are just starting to do that now. We also are implementing mentoring programs that will be a key part of our succession-planning process. The senior management team currently leads our succession-planning process by developing people below them. We also have heavy interaction with our board of directors on succession-planning for senior executive jobs.

Because agility is a key component of my strategy, I have tried to encourage our staff to be the same way. At weekly staff meetings we try to stay focused on what is changing, what is happening with our customers and competitors, and what needs to be done to protect our company and make it successful in the future.

That strategy has helped us recently because as soon as we saw the incident develop in the Gulf of Mexico with the BP blowout, we helped spearhead the formation of a coalition of shallow-water drilling companies (the Shallow Water Energy Security Coalition). We set up meetings in Washington, D.C., within days of the incident to start communicating with key congressional leaders and the Department of the Interior, guessing correctly that something was going to happen. Quite frankly, I believe we kept the shallow-water drilling business out of the drilling moratorium because we were able to communicate that the same safety concerns over deepwater drilling did not exist with us; there was no reason to have a moratorium that included shallow-water drilling. I think that adaptability and being able to react quickly helped us and helped our entire industry.

Tracking Accountability

We regularly use several performance indicators, and we use those to follow the progress of various initiatives and plans when the strategy changes. Even though the actual targets and metrics we use may change, the key drivers for our business are essentially the same. We have a simple business model in many ways; we provide offshore drilling rigs for the exploration and production companies that operate around the world. Our success is based on allocating the right drilling rig to each project, the utilization of those assets over time, and how much we are being paid each day to operate those drilling rigs.

I tell everybody at Seahawk Drilling that they are accountable for something; it does not matter what your job is, and, if for nothing else, you are accountable for your own performance. We make sure everybody knows what our strategy is and what their individual and team objectives and performance metrics are relative to our strategy and business plan. I think that is the key to building a performance ethic in a company.

Executive Collaboration

Keeping the collaborative approach in mind, our management team is close knit. My chief operating officer (COO) is focused primarily on our operations offshore, keeping the rigs running safely and properly crewed, and he spends much more time right now with customers than I do. He is focused on providing quality service to our customers. He and I speak almost daily and spend a significant amount of time together dealing with various business issues. The chief financial officer (CFO) and I have not worked together long, as he is new to the company. I have been spending more time with him talking about strategy, business plans, goals, and what we need to do from a financial standpoint to position the company for the future. Those are two key people within our management team.

Our general counsel is also a critical part of the management team. He is in charge of risk management, as well as legal and compliance, so I spend considerable time discussing our business and current issues with him. Rounding out the senior team are the head of human resources and the head of corporate development and planning. We all meet as a group at least once a week to talk about key issues and to make decisions; all of our meetings are action-oriented.

Additionally, I have a good relationship with our board of directors. I actually recruited everybody on the board, and while I was not personal friends with any of them, I knew about half of them ahead of time and during the recruitment process got to know them much better. Our goal was to develop a board that represented a variety of skills and that's what we have. My relationship with the directors is open and collaborative; I encourage the board members to communicate directly with my management team and to talk to anyone else they would like to within the company. It is important for public boards, in particular, to have access to all employees so that they can understand what is going on inside the company without having to go through the CEO first.

The process we have for translating the needs of the board and setting them into motion is simple. We involve a number of people in board meetings, other than the senior management team; the communication process starts there. The board is actively involved in our strategy development review sessions, our annual business planning sessions, and our quarterly performance reviews. Members have an opportunity to voice their opinions and ask questions during those meetings, and I encourage them to follow up with key individuals after the meetings if there are questions, instead of going through me. Giving the board direct access to key employees is a more effective way for boards to operate; it makes them an active part of the company instead of just people coming to board meetings to exercise their duties as directors.

Effective Communication

Effective communication is one of our key initiatives as a company; we focus on communication throughout the company so that everybody understands what his or her duties and goals are, and how they fit into the strategies and goals of the company as a whole.

One of our best practices for communicating effectively involves our leadership team communicating with key managers and teams on an ongoing basis, and we communicate directly with our employees through frequent employee meetings. Additionally, I spend time with customers, suppliers, and investors, so there is a good cross-section of communication going on; I encourage the rest of my management team to do the same.

I have worked at other companies before where the CEO was basically the only communicator, and all other employees were expected to just go and do their jobs. But we are a growing company, and we are trying to develop a culture that involves everyone in our success. It is important to communicate broadly, not just throughout the company, but also with all stakeholders, whether they are employees, customers, suppliers, investors, or directors on the board.

One of the things I do to ensure I am managing as a responsible leader is get feedback from the board, management, and employees. It is important to monitor what is going on—and what other people think is going on, as well. I also strive to instill within the company and our employees that as a management team, we have a commitment to them and, on a broader level, to the communities where we live and work. We are focused on ethical and fair behavior; there are no shortcuts to getting things done right, and we have a strong health, safety, and environmental culture here, as well.

Operating rigs offshore is our business, so safety is one of the key elements in our operating strategy, and it is central to our company culture. Our commitments to the community and the environment come down to being fair, being ethical, and making sure everybody in the company understands that there is nothing so important with our business that we will take any shortcuts in those areas. Also, I personally spend a great deal of time working with people in the community; I am on several charitable boards, and I am actively involved with those organizations. I encourage our employees to do the same by getting involved in the community, participating in what is going on, and trying to help out where they can.

Motivating our workforce is another element that relies on consistent communication. People who understand what their job is, what their individual goals are, and how all that fits into the success of the company tend to do better jobs. Therefore, we do the best we can to create opportunities for our employees to be successful, and we remain transparent about everything we do; we share as much information as possible with our employees within the constraints of what we can do as a public company. Everybody knows our strategy at the company; they know what our goals are and what our vision is. While we do offer monetary incentives and bonuses, they are secondary to communicating and making sure everyone understands what has to be done for our company to be successful.

To stay abreast of changes or trends that could affect us, communication is again key. We make sure we gather feedback and monitor information from many different places. This is one area we focus on at our weekly staff meetings, when we visit with our customers, and even when visiting with investors. We try to keep a close eye on what is happening that might affect our business, not just in Washington, but also with our customers and with our investors. The more information you have from different sources, the better prepared you will be when change occurs.

Building a Strong, Recognizable Capital Business

Return on investment (ROI) is an important metric for our business; how you allocate the capital you have as a company is important, particularly in a capital-intensive business like offshore drilling. A new shallow-water drilling rig costs in excess of $150 million; if we spend that kind of money on one drilling rig, it is important to be confident that we will get a good return on the investment we are making. The same thing applies if you allocate those assets to individual drilling projects; you want to make sure you continue to provide a good return on the investment you made.

We use other benchmarks besides ROI, such as return on capital employed. We try to break our corporate performance indicators into metrics for individual people and departments so they understand their actions have an impact on the return we produce as a company. When our investors place money in Seahawk, they expect to see an adequate return on their investment. For us to provide that, we must produce a solid ROI from the way we allocate that capital in our business decisions.

We are trying to encourage strong company recognition and build a robust brand identity at Seahawk right now. We want to be recognized for being quick to react to opportunities and threats. We have a real bias for action at Seahawk; we focus on teamwork, creating a healthy and safe work environment, and being performance-driven. We try to convey those attributes in our communications and actions. When we talk to customers, investors, or anyone else, we continue to focus on the same things we are talking about here. We are building a brand that says we are flexible and quick to take action, provide a safe working environment, and focus on operational excellence at all levels.

Words of Advice

The most important piece of advice I can share with other upcoming executives is to listen to other people. Nobody has all of the good ideas, so it is important to listen to others. They will also help give you an idea of how good a job you are doing.

The other piece of advice I can offer is to be ethical and fair in all situations; be courageous at times and don't be afraid to fail; and encourage the people who work for you to do the same.

The last thing I would tell up-and-coming executives is not to take themselves too seriously. I think personal hubris has killed the careers of more than one executive.

Key Takeaways

- The success of a business can sometimes be measured by how assets are allocated and utilized on projects and how much money they bring in during the project.
- Involve people at all levels of the organization when developing a business plan; communicate with them and make sure they develop their own action plans in concert with the overall strategy.
- Giving the board of directors direct access to key employees is a more effective way for the directors to operate; it makes them an active part of the business.
- Being adaptable and flexible, constantly trying to do a better job, and seeking feedback are all important components to being a successful executive.
- Return on investment (ROI), or how you allocate your capital, is a critical ingredient in the success of a capital-intensive business.

Randall D. (Randy) Stilley has served as Seahawk Drilling Inc.'s president and chief executive officer (CEO) since September 2008. Prior to joining Seahawk, Mr. Stilley was president and CEO of Hercules Offshore Inc. from October 2004 to June 2008. From January 2004 to October 2004, he was the CEO of Seitel Inc. Mr. Stilley was also president of the Oilfield Services Division at Weatherford International Inc. from 1997 to 2000. Prior to joining Weatherford, he served in a variety of positions at Halliburton Company.

Mr. Stilley is a registered professional engineer in the state of Texas and a member of the Society of Petroleum Engineers.

Mr. Stilley holds a Bachelor of Science degree in aerospace engineering from the University of Texas at Austin.

Leadership in a Multifaceted Company

Harmon B. Miller

President and Chief Executive Officer

Miller Zell Inc.

ASPATORE

The Role of the CEO

I am the president and chief executive officer (CEO) of Miller Zell, a leader in strategic retail design and consulting representing all disciplines of retail, including design, store implementation, shopper marketing, consumer insights, and retail research and analysis. I own the large majority of the company, which I founded more than thirty years ago.

In my role as CEO, I am responsible for developing the plans and programs we are implementing as we evolve. We deal with several large companies and enjoy a twenty-year relationship with one of the world's largest retailers, which is impressive in itself. Almost all the visual communication a customer sees in this particular retail environment was designed and manufactured, and in many cases installed, by Miller Zell. We perform similar services for other large clients, and we have been fortunate in establishing relationships with some top-tier companies. We provide what goes inside a store—what the shopper sees and what gives the shopper information about the merchandise.

We are unique in that we may be the only $100 billion business sector that is completely fragmented.

We provide internal design, store renovation programs, and the ongoing in-store promotional programs, which are separate businesses. We are working on developing comprehensive programs beyond the scope of competitors. We have several competitors; we have competition in strategy, in design, and in developing and producing materials in retail stores. To our knowledge no other company provides as wide a range of integrated services and products as we do.

My role has changed somewhat over the years, but a better way to view it is that it has evolved as much as it has simply changed. My duties have remained consistent over the past several years, which is typical of many entrepreneurial companies where the founder has taken the lead in growing the company. I anticipate that my role will remain consistent, but as the company has grown, we are developing some top-tier management at the C-level. We have people in the various areas of strategies and creative design, which is a strong part of our business. We manufacture large-format print, an area in which we are a leader. We provide installation services for permanent and promotional materials. Our surveys have indicated that fewer than half of the promotional materials that go into retail stores are installed, which is a loss of business opportunity, so one of our most distinguishing features is that we offer a complete package, from design through installation.

C-Level Management

About three years ago, I appointed a chief operating officer (COO) and a chief financial officer (CFO), who is responsible for anything that is manufactured and for services provided. We also have a chief marketing officer (CMO). These C-level managers have their own management teams. We have been stable in the senior management positions at Miller Zell, but we are also hiring certain types of people now, as we provide a broader range of services to our clients.

To ensure that the company's goals are being met, we set specific goals with each of our C-level managers and review those goals, from where we are now to how we are growing over the next three months, during our monthly meetings. In setting those goals, we provide both revenue and a profit goal for each of them. For instance, the recent economic downturn has been difficult for many industries and companies, but we were profitable consistently throughout that period.

Although we may revise goals from time to time, we do not change our strategy. We provide an integrated network of products and services for our clients, and we will not change that, though we do not provide our full array of services for every client. Sometimes we start small and then build trust and a relationship, in much the same manner as a successful advertising agency deals with its clients. Often they receive a series of projects from a new client that they do well, and from that, they pick up the entire account. That is the model we use in our specific areas of expertise.

Keeping Track of Progress

We have weekly Executive Committee meetings where we discuss, among other topics, our monthly profit and loss statement. The operating group has a weekly planning meeting, which I periodically attend, and we have a quarterly senior management meeting to assess how we are doing.

Because the areas of expertise covered by the senior management team require various skills (e.g., finance people do not have the same skills as marketing people, and the manufacturing people have yet another skill set), each of the managers has different goals, which are set for them and developed with me. I review what we have been doing over the last few years and then set goals that are aggressive and require us to stretch.

Judging by our low turnover rate, I feel we have a satisfied workforce. A key element to that is our recruiting. We are good at recruiting the kind of people we want to have. We hold two large meetings a year where the other senior managers and I tell the staff what is happening and provide an update about what we are planning to do over the next six months to a year.

Leadership Style

My leadership style is based on trust and openness. When we set goals for our employees, we make them clearly measurable so that employees know exactly how they are doing. I have an open-door policy; any employee at any level can come in and talk with me. Much of that communication takes place among the senior managers. I have learned much through my reading, and I continuously flow that information to the appropriate people in the rest of the company.

I write a large quantity of memos about what we ought to be doing, which I send to the appropriate people, asking them to reflect on my thoughts and give me their opinions. I also find and send around good articles that are relevant to various parts of the business. We have a top management meeting monthly where we evaluate what we are doing and the goals we have set for ourselves. All of these avenues of communication have helped me stay connected with every facet of the business.

We are constantly expanding our relationships with existing clients, which include some of the biggest companies in the business, while establishing relationships with other major accounts, particularly retailers. About 90 percent of our total revenue comes from retailers of one form or another, and we have clients, such as consumer product providers, that serve retailers.

Community Involvement

Atlanta is a great city with a good reputation. The city has always had strong business leaders, and I am pleased to contribute to the city's reputation. As our company has grown, I have realized it was time for me to be more actively involved in the community, so I am now active in significant charities and on the board of directors of the Atlanta Opera. As with every other opera board, (including the Met in New York), we are looking for money, so I help out with certain aspects of that. I am also using my business acumen in helping the organization run more efficiently to make the best use of the funds we develop.

As a company, we are becoming more actively involved with environmental issues. Our graphics plant has done an excellent job of greening their operations. We are aided in our efforts by the city administration, which has set strict guidelines for environmental compliance.

Motivation

Compensation is always a motivating factor for employees, but it is not the only one. We give our employees the opportunity to grow, which is one of the most important things we provide. When our employees perceive that they have an opportunity to grow and that the company is a growing company, we retain the right types of people. We also have one other valuable motivating factor—the companies we do business with. Our employees are proud of the work we do with these large organizations.

We also offer opportunities for personal growth for all of our employees. For instance, a person in the graphics center can do well and get promoted to supervisor and then to a top manager position there. As with certain other industries, our most heavily compensated people are in sales. Some of our people look for outside areas to earn extra income, and we are open to that. We also have latitude in transferring between departments, which helps create added opportunities for the employees.

Building Client Trust

One of the worst situations for us is having a client that cannot make a decision because if the client cannot decide, nothing happens. We are seeing some instances of that hesitation now in the tough economy. Clients are asking themselves whether they should take a relatively inexpensive approach, such as upgrading existing stores, rather than a more aggressive approach, such as opening several new stores and expanding into new business areas.

These decisions are often delayed; if a client decides to open four stores instead of ten, the cost per store will be higher. We are fortunate that most of our clients have been with us for a long time, so there is a significant amount of trust between us. We are in a position where we can counsel and advise our clients, and they trust us.

Part of the trust we have built with our clients stems from longevity, and our employees play a critical role in establishing, maintaining, and growing our relationships. One of the most important aspects of my job is ensuring that we are both growing our talent, particularly at the senior management level, and periodically bringing in high-quality new people. We were able to maintain our employee longevity even through the recession; we had concluded about eighteen months ago that because we had a strong balance sheet, we would do everything possible to avoid layoffs, and we succeeded. Such a move required a significant investment on our part, and it was well received. It has been an important factor in retaining people as the economy has started to turn around.

Flexibility as a Part of Leadership

We stress agility as a part of our strategy, but that is within the context of setting goals that are agreed to by people and monitored. However, though we set goals, there will always be change in the marketplace. For instance, one of our largest clients decided to get out of the retail business without notifying us first. The move required us to change and be flexible, which was aided by the fact that we are always bringing in new clients.

As CEO, I must stay abreast of trends and changes that can affect the company. In addition to my reading, which includes traditional business publications and industry magazines, as well as books, I also attend outside senior management meetings that are relevant to our business. We are a member of the American Association of Advertising Agencies, and we were the first company that was not a true advertising agency invited to join. That organization has been invaluable in helping me stay current on below-the-line activities.

Something I have learned in my experience is that you can never do anything yesterday. I always wish I could do better as CEO; in some areas, I have missed out, and in others I have been successful. The best practice I have learned is that if things are not working out the way they are supposed to, you have to change them. I think we do a pretty good job of that. I seek feedback from my employees through our various meetings. We also have many occasions to sit down and talk candidly about the opportunities that are presenting themselves in their direct area or a related area.

Encouraging Strong Company Recognition

Three years ago we had little interest in presenting Miller Zell publicly. One of my employees observed that we had reached a size where we were going to be defined, so we had better do it ourselves, or someone would do it for us, and we might not like the results. That observation made me realize we needed to engage in a public relations (PR) program.

For example, if we have something interesting or important to say, which we frequently do, we make sure it is quoted in various business publications. We have used our marketing department for this PR effort, but the effort includes other departments, as well.

Today our PR program covers something fundamental to this business—that is, how people see us. We are in the business of helping retail businesses present themselves in the best possible way, and we reached a point where we needed to do the same for ourselves. As a result, the program could not be simply a marketing plan. It has reached every area of the business, including operations.

Lessons Learned

CEOs need to know the businesses they are in. If they are doing something innovative, they can write the script for themselves, but it is important to have the support of good people who can do their jobs well at all levels. It is tempting to spend too much time in the early days of developing a business with too much planning and not enough doing.

Key Takeaways

- You can never do anything yesterday. If things are not working out the way they are supposed to, don't be afraid to change them.
- If you have something interesting or important to say, make sure it is quoted in various business publications. The marketing department is important for PR efforts, but other departments play key roles, as well. Your presentation is fundamental to the business because it is how your clients and prospects see you.
- Compensation is always a motivating factor for employees, but it is not the only one. Growth opportunities are one of the most important things you offer to your staff. If they see they have an opportunity to grow and that the company is a growing company, then you will retain the right types of people.
- CEOs need to know the businesses they are in. If they are doing something innovative, they can write the script for themselves, but it is important to have the support of good people who can do good jobs. It is tempting to spend too much time developing a business plan and not enough doing.

A native of Tacoma, Washington, Harmon B. (Sandy) Miller migrated east to Atlanta as a young child and attended Emory University, where he earned a Bachelor of Arts degree in economics. After finishing his tour of duty in the U.S. Army, in 1974 he purchased a small screen-printing company in Atlanta. He quickly began to add capability after capability to create a vertically integrated visual design strategy and a retail implementation company second to none.

Mr. Miller, president and chief executive officer of Miller Zell Inc., has always been a driven visionary who saw the world of retail as an industry ripe with opportunity to better showcase brands and influence consumers at the true point of decision—the retail shelf. Propelled by his vision to provide a wide array of visual and marketing services to retailers, he followed his entrepreneurial spirit and set out to create the leading retail strategy/design/implementation company.

Today, Miller Zell is distinguished as a leading provider of world-class selling environments for major retailers and large branded consumer manufacturing companies. Miller Zell focuses on helping companies define their retail selling spaces by providing renovation services, as well as new store design and complete turn-key implementation services.

With a blue-chip client base that includes multi-national corporate titans like Walmart, Cirque du Soleil, ExxonMobil, and Citizens Bank, Miller Zell continues to evolve as a company that has a resource set second to none. From its state-of-the-art large-format and digital printing division to its industry-decorated strategy and design department, Miller Zell bases the core of its business in a five-building campus in the western Atlanta suburbs.

With Miller Zell offices in Atlanta, New York, Toronto, Arkansas, and China, Mr. Miller continues in his quest to provide retailers and branded manufacturers with the ability to open stores faster and more productively. Because changes to the store are imminently more measurable than other forms of mass-media marketing, Miller Zell strives to provide its clients with better retail solutions that garner measurably better business results.

Building Communities through Collaborative Leadership and Adherence to Strategic Viability

George W. Hamlin IV

President and Chief Executive Officer

Canandaigua National Bank and Trust,
Canandaigua National Corporation

ASPATORE

Introduction

We are a traditional community bank (1887) redesigned to deliver comprehensive financial services to individuals, be they growing families or businesses. That is, through education and advice, facilitated by financial products and services, we strive to be the "primary care physician" for financial matters: access to credit (liquidity against owned assets), depository and transfer/payment, investment management, fiduciary services, and for client/customers: financial planning, private banking, and online brokerage services.

As chief executive officer (CEO), my primary role is to listen, question, observe, advise, and guide colleagues to ensure alignment with our current fifteen-year strategic plan 2020, core values, and mission. Our senior management group is highly competent, and each has major responsibilities:

- Chief enterprise risk management officer (corporate counsel, human resources, audit, credit administration, and compliance)
- Chief finance officer (finance, operations [information technology, account operations] and asset management liability committee [ALCO], liquidity, capital management)
- Chief commercial services officer (commercial lending, commercial services, etc.)
- Chief retail services officer (retail and mortgage lending, CEO CNB Mortgage)
- Branch administration (sales and service operations)
- WSG (wealth strategies group—trusts and estates [T&E] fiduciary services, investment management, financial planning)
- Chief CVM officer (Integrated relationship, customer value management over all of the above customer/client services for the entire holding company CNC, assuring an integrated, quality customer/client experience)

Qualifications and prior experience were diverse and those of a generalist. I have degrees in physics (BS) and law (JD) and earned a living at first as an Air Force fighter pilot (F-105) for nearly six years during Viet Nam. After law school and practicing law (T&E, tax, and corporate) for ten years, I joined the bank and after a year assumed the role as CEO of Canandaigua National Bank and Trust (CNB), etc., for thirty-one years to date. This was supplemented very modestly in financial terms but to an enormous degree in experiential learning terms as a professional actor for nearly twenty years mostly at the Bristol Valley Theater, an established summer stock company in Naples, New York. My uncle asked me (twice) to come to the bank (then $80 million in assets), the second time as VP, counsel and "trainee" as his eventual successor in a "couple" of years. It was one year; I was thirty-seven years old; and what a ride it has been!

Traditional Banking: The "Oil" of Commerce

By way of an analogy, most people understand that oil performs an essential function in the engines of their automobiles, but is not top of mind, taken pretty much for granted. Most are probably more alert to running out of gas than noting the oil pressure or checking whether they are running out of oil. But I know from my experiences as a fighter and commercial pilot for forty-eight years to date that if it doesn't have oil, the engine *will* seize.

Main Street community banking is to commerce as oil is to an engine. Long before there was a Wall Street, commerce was facilitated by banking—from the beginning of human history. The media have been focusing on the big, bad banks and their big, bad bonuses because 85 percent of the banking assets are held by the largest 100 banks or so. People assume that if they are addressing 85 percent of the money, they are addressing 100 percent of the problem. For too many folks the word "bank" has become a four-letter word, a pejorative term. The fact remains, however, that 7,960 banks had virtually nothing to do with originating sub-prime mortgages or precipitating the financial debacle that followed. Unfortunately, people don't know the differences among a commercial (savings) bank, an investment bank, and a credit union (bank), and I can understand that. One difference is, though, that a commercial bank pays federal and state income taxes, and the other two do not, either because they no longer exist or they just don't (exempt politically).

Community banks (7,960 strong) represent 15 percent of the banking assets spread across 90 percent of the land mass of America. They did not cause the financial crisis, but were victimized by it, along with their customers. Nor did we seize up in October 2008, like Wall Street's commercial paper market and overnight interbank lending among money center banks, because we operate under a business model distinctly different from that of Wall Street.

The media reported the widely held view, "We have to fix Wall Street so Main Street can have access to small business commercial and retail loans and mortgages, student loans, etc." Pardon me! While we may be relatively small, we not only kept the pace, open for business as usual, but also tripled the pace of loan activity, deposit growth, and earnings, returning record levels of earnings per share in the history of the company over the period of the crisis from 2007 through 2009. Main Street banking kept the funds flowing and the engine of commerce well lubricated without missing a beat. We did not restrict or change our credit standards; any creditworthy small business was open to us. True, the sensible borrower was reticent to leverage up in the face of lower business demand and a prediction of a turbulent time ahead. But the system was awash in liquidity.

Canandaigua National's Background

Unfortunately, many people, whose primary information about banking comes from the media, are tragically ignorant about the importance of banking to the essential welfare of all of society. Just because they have a bank account, they think they know the inner workings of the system. So, here's a quick overview of our bank: We have $1.6 billion in assets and a $1.6 billion under investment management in our Wealth Strategies Group, so we are now a company of $3.2 billion in assets (under management) with total revenues of $100 million in 2009. Thirty years ago, we were an $80-million community bank with an equal size trust department. In the last ten years, we have tripled the size of the bank's assets and quadrupled its earnings.

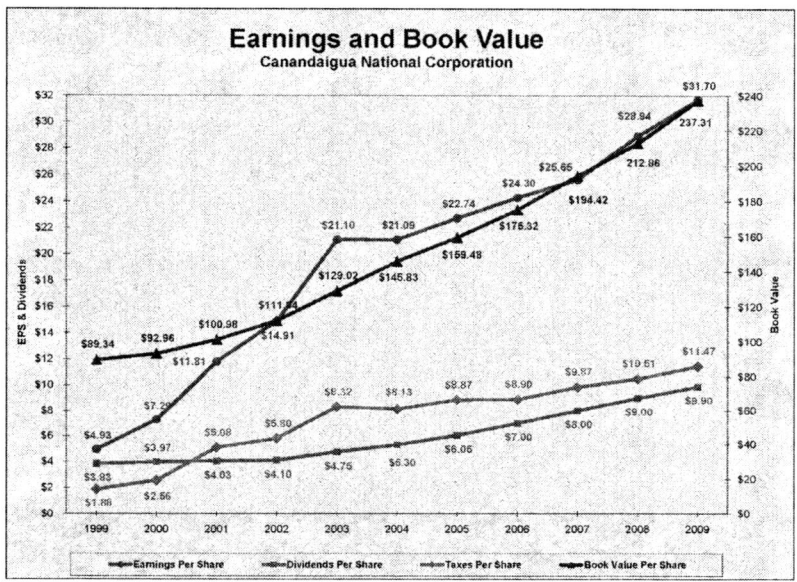

We have done it with an asset quality that is enviable and a net charge-off rate on the order of 20 basis points, which is one-fifth of a percent.

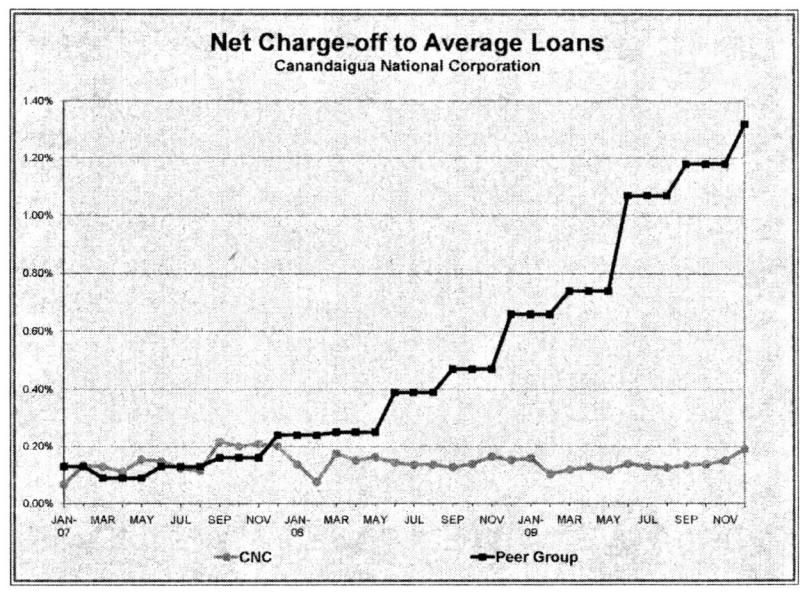

Our great strength is due to our history of reliable, sustained earnings, retained earnings, and capital (common equity) growth. Therefore, we have been able to do essentially as we want, regardless of what world markets, Congress, or governments do. We can do this because by strategic intention we maintained the simplest of balance sheets. As the community's financial intermediary, we lend deposits gathered from the community back into the community. Our number-one mission is to grow the community, and our number-two mission is to optimize and not maximize our earnings. We spread them among our four constituents: the shareholders, our staff, our client base, and, by extension, the community at large.

Although we are a public company, one of our strengths is that we are not publicly traded and, hence, not subject to the instabilities of speculation on our stock in the market, which can get very removed from the underlying economics and purposes of the enterprise. The real growth of a company is reflected in its retained earnings, equity balance sheet, history of earnings, quality of management, quality of products, and prospects for the future.

Even during the tumultuous period between 2007 and 2009, the community banking model remained safe and secure. During that three-year period, in fact, we put in the very best earnings and had the very best credit quality. *US Banker* magazine for the second year ranked us nineteenth of the top 200 community banks in the country, which puts us in the top one-quarter of the top one percent of all commercial banks in the country based on not one, not two, but three years of return on equity, which in 2009 was 14.58 percent. (This also happens to be the average return for each of the three years of performance.) This dramatically shows that our approach works for all seasons of the financial cycle. In each of the last five recessions since 1973 we actual grew on average 12 percent for all major elements: deposits, loans, and earnings.

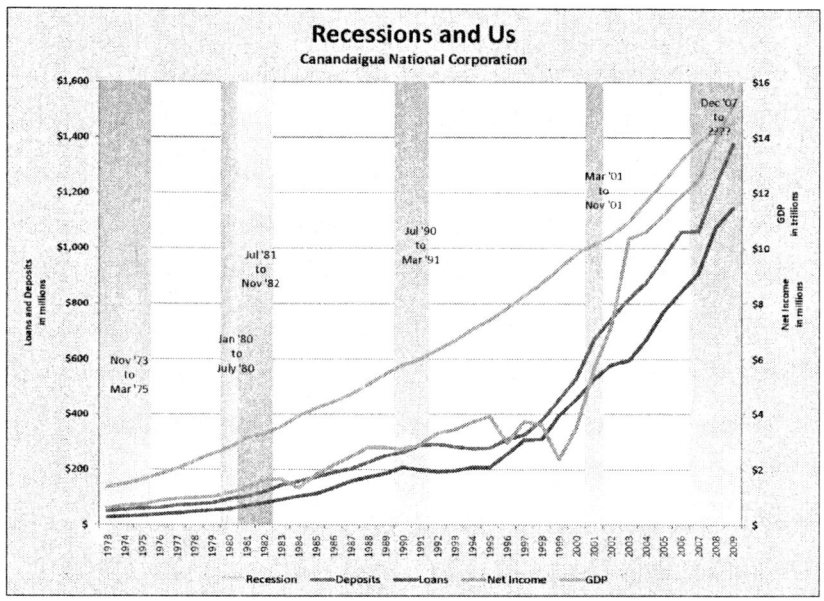

We began as a small community bank in Canandaigua, twenty-five miles southeast of Rochester, New York, and starting in 1998 eventually embraced all of Rochester Metropolitan Statistical Area (MSA), with twenty-eight offices in the two-county area. Now, we are acknowledged as *the* community bank of Rochester.

Many ask why we're called Canandaigua Bank when we're actually Rochester's bank. I remember meeting Sandy Weill, the founder of Citigroup, during a bank forum in which I was asked to participate at the Waldorf Astoria in New York City in the early 1990s. The topic was expanded financial services (insurance and securities) for the banking industry. Tom Le Breck, president of Chase, and I representing banks small and large, and Sandy and Hank Greenberg representing Travelers (Securities) and AIG (insurance), respectively, were on the stage. It was a friendly audience—because of the demographic, there were obviously more representatives from community banks in the audience than larger institutions. I was moved to say that if you can spell "Canandaigua" and pronounce "Canandaigua," that implies an infinity upon which a business relationship can be built.

Fast forward four or five years, when I was the small-bank member on the Federal Reserve Bank of New York Board. The new incoming large-bank representative was Mr. Weill, so I went over to reintroduce myself. He looked at me and, without even blinking an eye, said, "Canandaigua—if you can spell it and pronounce it, then that implies an infinity on which a business relationship can be built." My teeth nearly fell out of my mouth in amazement that this man, who had just created the largest bank in the country by merging Travelers and Citibank, remembered my impromptu, throw-away line from five years earlier. We became friends; he is an amazing man, who apparently has never forgotten anything, with an inspiring outlook and passion for building organizations. *The Deal*, his memoir, was never, ever about the money, but always about the company of people who drove his success, and that is precisely the focus of our operations—our collaboration between our staff and client/customers—the embodiment of the value of our company, more accurately said.

The Emotional Component of Banking

In my experience, I have observed that, even though the banking business is perceived to be about numbers and ratios, two-thirds or more of the business is actually about how people feel about the numbers. This emotion was dramatically demonstrated between 2007 and 2009, when the world markets lost confidence and fell into panic, which history shows they do fairly regularly—eighteen times, in fact, over the last 200 years.

In spite of all the social and political debate, economics is actually a social science, part the science of money and numbers and more than an even part about the psychology of how we feel about those numbers. Whether it concerns jobs, security, return on investment, or products and services, economics is an objective manifestation of human activity. Our job is to observe and understand that it works in a quasi-scientific environment so that we can construct laws and constraints that will curb the harmful effects of human irrationality on the system—the "animal spirits," as coined by John Maynard Keynes (*The General Theory of Employment, Interest, and Money*, Macmillan, 1936). George A. Akerlof and Robert J. Shiller in their book (*Animal Spirits: How Human Psychology Drives the Economy and Why It Matters for Global Capitalism*, Princeton University Press, 2009) have emphasized how the noneconomic and irrational emotional influences on market and human behavior traditionally have been discounted far too much and now are acknowledged to have been much more significant than previously supposed.

Economists Assumptions & Response

Understanding motivation and the human response.

	A	B
	Economic Rational	Economic Not Rational
C	Non Economic Rational	D Non Economic Not Rational

Human component is the biggest variable.
"A" represents classic analysis— this leaves out 75% of the possibilities!

Roles and Responsibilities of a Community Bank CEO

As the CEO of our company, a community bank, I am left to focus on the roles of overall performance, planning, policies, public and government relations, and nurturing the culture of collaboration among our four constituencies. Ultimately, the sustainability of our company rests on my shoulders, and as such, I am the keeper of the vision, strategic plan, and, yes, the holy grail, if you will. Frankly, I am mostly overhead, but with my gaze fixed on the horizon, as I do not currently manage the details of opening, maintaining, or closing any investments or ensure that the bank is in compliance with required regulations. I liken my role to that of an orchestra conductor who selects the repertoire, ports of call, and perhaps even the musical interpretation. However, it is the music produced by the musicians that people come to hear. The "music" that is produced by our members is the synthesis of a beautiful collaboration of committed, well-educated, and thoughtful human beings. They come together voluntarily each day and perform an activity that they are passionate about and must do as a matter of their life's compulsion.

On a side note, I spent nearly twenty years as a professional member (in character roles) of a long-running summer stock company, The Bristol Valley Theater in Naples, New York, and currently I am actually the chairman of the Eastern School of Music from which our youngest son (thirty-three) graduated in 2000. I have been graced by my many insights gained as an actor and my associations with the arts and have applied artistic approaches and methods of communication to the development, design, and presentation of all of our bank's branches.

This is done for the purpose of "telling our story" through our architecture and people, as stage settings and actors do through a play or musical. We tend to focus and reflect the history of the area surrounding of our offices, thereby reaching out and identifying with the human elements of each community in a personal way. I have even used actors to convey customers' concerns and interests to help human resources (HR) show our people in a live way what they could encounter, as well as to employ them to reinforce the elements and themes of our culture through the design and production of the year's celebrations and staff gatherings by use of stories and activities. People remember stories, not PowerPoint lists and presentations. When the scientist's left brain can embrace the art world's right brain, wonderful inspirations can happen. Because I focus on fostering such collaboration, my leadership approach is entirely different from those of most people in my position.

Risk Exposure: The Large-Bank versus Community-Bank Models

Philosophically speaking, business enterprises can be characterized by the degree of risk they take, choose to take, or must take because of circumstances beyond their control. Most events are beyond our control; if we think we are in control of our destiny, nothing could be further from the truth, but such a harmless delusion may allow us to sleep better at night.

At Canandaigua National, we choose to have a simple balance sheet consisting of lending deposits drawn from the community that find their way back into the community in the form of loans. We also provide demand payment services, such as checking accounts, electronic funds transfers (i.e., debit cards), and investments that we manage and trade for the accounts of individual and institutional clients.

Large Wall Street institutions choose a complex balance sheet that includes the same banking elements that our Main Street bank provides, as well as significantly more risky ventures related to investment banking, proprietary trading on their own accounts (as opposed to the accounts of third-party customers), and underwriting of new complex derivative instruments. Now, these choices are deliberate, and in normal times, the performance of these larger institutions has been spectacular, especially in recent years. But we now have seen what can happen with such huge risk exposure to the vagaries of financial markets. Even though the new innovative financial investment contracts were purported to diversify and limit risk, owing to the unintended consequences that accompany such innovations, they actually concentrated that exposure in one large company—AIG, the largest insurance company conglomerate in the world.

The values of those new instruments were ravaged by speculators run amuck and propelled by the loss of confidence and panic that gripped the markets. When it was finally recognized that the valuations of these new instruments were plagued with uncertainty, this set off a process of dramatic and punishing discounting leading to widespread margin calls. Along the way, investors also discovered that the investments were highly leveraged. Because this practice was repeated elsewhere in the world, the markets in every country of the world became as vulnerable as tinder waiting for a single spark to come drifting in from a firestorm in California or wherever.

Because we chose to maintain a simple balance sheet, Canandaigua National had virtually no exposure to this volatility common to the financial markets, which proved to be an important feature in our favor. Our choice kept us safe and sound and above the chaos and ruinous exposure that ultimately resulted in the demise of an industry, the investment banking industry.

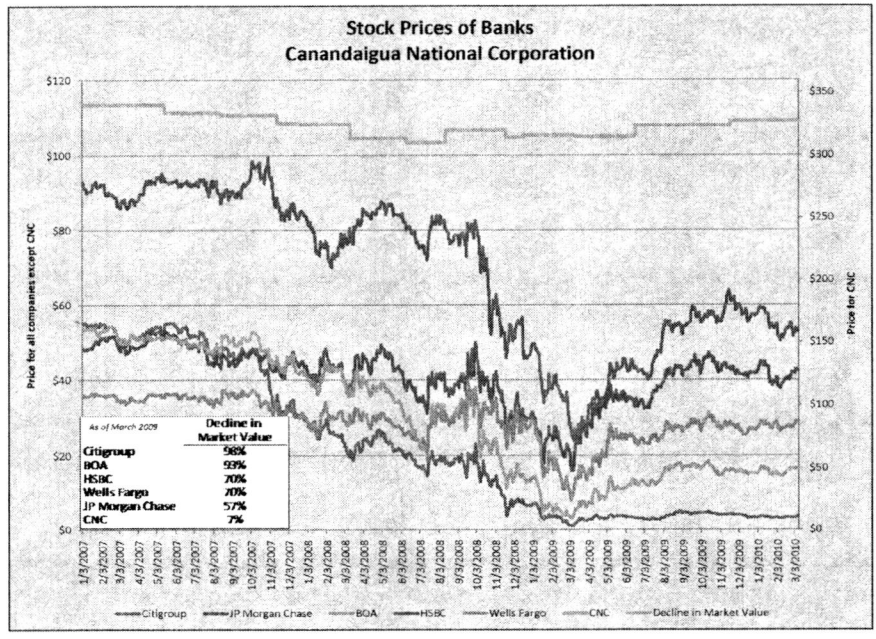

However, our situation was no accident, but rather resulted from a deliberate choice to, first and foremost, focus on building the community and improving the welfare of our client customers. We focus on developing mutually beneficial relationships based on supporting community enterprises through financial services and access to capital, education, and advice. Where the principal largest banks lost 50 percent to 98 percent of their market value at the bottom, our stock was virtually unaffected and held firm.

Managing for Long-Term Growth, Not Short-Term Gain

We also share approximately 30 percent of our current earnings in the form of a dividend. Fifty years ago, the amount of this dividend pretty much determined the value of your stock. Today, however, it's determined by the growth of net equity that is calculated based on retained earnings after dividends and taxes added to the common equity of the enterprise. These retained earnings build capital. (Incidentally, the capital in our company mathematically doubles every seven to eight years.)

Most of Wall Street, on the other hand, focuses on enhancing shareholder value through the short-term realization of the valuation on the sale of stock. However, the stock price does not necessarily reflect the true value of the underlying company or the growth of its business, especially if you water the company's effect down by combining it with fifty to 100 issues making up the modern mutual fund. This may be a wonderful way to diversify, but it does take your eye off the ball of what is happening to the individual company's balance sheet, earnings statement, and underlying business and growth.

Such a preoccupation with price generally has led to adopting short-term exit strategies where all or parts of companies are merged or sold out completely, thereby achieving the primary goal of capturing immediate value, rather than incrementally gathering it over many years. We, on the other hand, share 30 percent of our earnings, year over year, and thereby preserve the value of the dynamic human collaboration that is the foundation of the value of our company, as well as all real productivity that occurs in our economy for that matter. Such growth sustains us all, citizens and government alike.

In stark contrast to the banking industry's oft-cited overriding purpose to make money at every turn, our primary mission is to grow the community at large by supporting its constituents. We strive to optimize and not maximize our earnings so that we can share the benefits from our daily collaborations with our greater community. We do this not only because it is the right thing to do, but also because the vitality of our enterprise and community is interdependent. Growing the community fosters the bank's own growth and our increased financial strength, which in turn promotes the growth of the community. It's a full circle.

The Community Bank as "Midwife" of Human Productivity—the Principal Cause of Commerce

If philosophy, values, and culture constitute an organization's type and character, then it follows that a CEO whose style is compatible with those attributes would be its most effective leader. The community bank is a special business enterprise because it deals with a broader scope of concern and more diverse constituents than other financial institutions, or even most other businesses, for that matter. As I was recently explaining to our employees, we don't have to care about what Congress or other banks are doing because we have been doing this for a long time, and we are the ones that are thriving and growing.

But consider this, I suggest: we are the ones that actually create the "money" itself, and that amount is what we record on the accounts of the bank. It is what we say it is.

Consider that when we close a loan for $100,000, we typically do so by making a deposit of that $100,000 into the borrower's account at the bank. The money supply has just been increased by the addition of that $100,000 that now appears in the account. When the $100,000 is spent to build or refurbish the house, for example, this disbursement fosters about $300,000 to $400,000 of economic activity—the so-called multiplier effect. That is the magic of banking; we, not the government, "mint the gold" we use to acquire our goods and services that we need to underwrite our families and businesses. We serve as the "midwife," as we bring to life money itself, but also in facilitating the financial structure for human productivity, which is the source of all commerce. Commerce builds into the economy, which then produces salaries, wages, benefits, houses, and autos, as well as cash flow that is subject to income and property taxes. Taxes underwrite fees for government enterprises and benefits, which in turn make happy citizens who vote 98 percent of the time for keeping the incumbent in office for yet another term.

As the midwife of this birthing process, we have been working since 3 a.m. in the wee hours of the morning, supporting the ingenuity and productivity of human beings. Then the government shows up about 10:30 in the morning with a cup of coffee, and the people think the money came from the government's largess, even though it is manufactured by banks. In fact, on December 31, 2009, we wrote a check for $11.7 million to the Federal Deposit Insurance Corporation (FDIC) to pay for three years of FDIC assessments in advance, up front—never before done. The usual way is to spread the burden over six years.

Now, the government is not paying the freight here—the banks are, out of their earnings and capital. It is not that this is not the right course to follow, but it is rude not to acknowledge what we are doing, bailing out the FDIC; we are providing the juice (or the "oil," if you will) that keeps the engine of commerce lubricated and running and that forms the basis for our economy and the tax base that funds government spending and benefits—Social Security, health care, etc. That is why we are a part of the DNA of society—*essential*.

Leadership Strategies

I utilize a consensus-style approach. My uncle recruited me to understudy with him as Canandaigua National's president to learn the ropes when I was thirty-seven. At first, because I knew nothing about banking, I wondered on what his judgment was based and inquired as to the method of his "madness." But he said, "We have a lot of people at the bank that know about banking, but you have perspective." So now, I'm thinking that my leadership style is based on the fact that I came in not knowing anything, the advantages of not harboring any prejudices (outmoded) about the subject matter itself.

This was also somewhat analogous to how I began as a fighter pilot. I listened very, very carefully to what my sergeant, whom I outranked, but who knew more about the mechanics of airplanes than I did, had to say as my crew chief. After all, I was going to rely on him to get me into the combat target area and back in one piece.

We employ 450 souls at Canandaigua National, of whom seventy-five are part-time. In the final analysis they know more about what they do day-to-day than I do and are quite talented in executing those many tasks. I listen carefully, since they know better how to improve on the task.

While they know the task and its content, it is my job to understand the environment and context of how these activities fit together and what is on the horizon, what we are trying to do, and how we will manage through the swamp of Congress's interventions. My job is to ensure that our "musicians" are safe and sound and can continue to do their magic by keeping one eye on the horizon and the other on our home plate.

So my style is to listen well and design the strategic plan to fit our goals, which are principally to add value to the customer relationship and not get bogged down psychologically by the mountain of compliance concerns that attends our business. These compliance concerns add no strategic value to our core business on which our vitality depends and which sustains us for the long term, potentially indefinitely as part of the DNA of the society we serve.

Everything we do is a matter of good business practice, which makes sense for all financial seasons. Virtually all of the regulations governing our industry are drawn up in a moment of crisis, at best a spot solution good for a snapshot in time, and thus obsolete almost the moment the ink has dried. Mostly they actually are not even applicable much after about three to six months because everyone (the markets and we) subject to them has moved on.

Central planning was repudiated with the fall of the Berlin Wall and the Communist system, its chief sponsor. It was a system that produced products no one wanted to buy. It is a static model not attuned to the free market influences of continuous change. Regulation is incremental central planning. We are a dynamic model, constantly changing as each transaction is closed by nimbly adapting to improve upon the next opportunity and so that we can add value and thereby stay relevant to our customers and the marketplace. Our ability to adapt and be nimble is our strength in this modern and ever changing world.

We developed a diagram hung on the wall of our HR department, which we share with every new employee—an inverted pyramid. The people who address the customers, who are on the bottom of most pyramids, are at the top of our pyramid, and the board of directors and I are at the point, buried in the ground at the bottom. We are, simply, the least significant compared to those who actually do the adding of value to the customer relationship.

While all of the corporate world and its MBAs and theorists think a company's success depends on who is at the top, I think the directors' role is to keep a watchful eye on objective events, the strategic plan, and the Holy Grail. They are very bright people, but they are not the executives or the specialists, and they only come in once a month. I sit on two hospital boards, and, even though I have a hand in the finances and strategic direction of the institutions, you don't want me to perform surgery on you. The directors may supervise on behalf of the shareholders, but the executive team is responsible for executing business propositions adroitly.

Our strategic plans span fifteen years (not three) because they are based on the notion that our economic cycles last ten years plus or minus two. Our capital planning projections extend from twenty to thirty years. We establish goals during strategic planning sessions that don't involve just twelve people, but the gang of forty (which really manages to be eighty) that includes virtually every leader and office manager. We meet three times a year for two days, which is possible because the bank is run by tellers and floor officers. I have never run into any organization that does fifteen-year strategic plans, and we are into our second, which extends through 2020.

Community Banking, an Enduring Business Model

It is our profits, retained earnings, and ultimately our capacity to restore, refresh, and grow our common equity by our retained earnings with sustained diverse revenues that are the key to our long-term sustainability and in keeping with our long-term commitment and mission to grow the community indefinitely. This is contrary to the more usual practice observed in the industry over the last three decades, which was to sell out or merge and thereby join in the continued consolidation of our industry. We have the resources and have dedicated ourselves to the "road less travelled," to stay the course in pursuit of our mission indefinitely. We will do this through collaboration of customers and clients, staff, colleagues, shareholders, and committed owners dedicated to the cause, and the community at large to provide comprehensive financial services (for "fun and profit") to individuals, growing families, and businesses.

We will do this first by taking an interest in our clients and then conveying that interest by action or deed, by listening to their stories, and by asking questions. We will let the clients talk, to tell us what their needs or challenges are; after all, we learn more by listening than by talking. Once we understand what is on their minds, we can know our customers' commitments and concerns. Only then can we know their needs and wants, allowing us to construct a set of solutions applying our products and services. We can explain these to them, using their own words to enhance their understanding and through a process of offering education and advice to solve their problems. By this approach, we will enhance their situations, thereby building on the relationship and ultimately leading to their peace of mind based on trust. Human matters trump business affairs; relationships trump transactions!

As we look to the future, our prospects are bright because our credit quality remains good and our earnings strong. Our local economy is historically highly diversified and has been designated by the financial press as being in the top twenty most resilient economies in the country, referring to its recovery potential. We know by history that the government intervention to re-regulate is at best a *static* exercise, representing a design addressing that which is truly just a "snapshot" of the moment in time. True, the regulations will take years to write, so some matters will remain open and uncertain, but my review of the Conferees' Reports reveals for the most part that we will be free to continue our business in the manner of our choosing. This is, of course, always the first concern conjured by the early drafts of such broad legislation, which had yet to be curtailed by an astonishing 400 amendments, and which generally eliminate most of the insanity that accompanies the opening blast of such legacy legislation.

This by no means minimizes the work and expense burden of complying with the myriad of new details that spring from this legislation. Regulations and their implementation and the cost of compliance will be significant. We have an imaginative staff, and I expect we will be able to legitimately work around any substantive road blocks that interfere with our ability to add value to the customer relationship. This I am sure we can manage because for the most part, these new requirements merely codified good business practices, which we already employ. We lament that we have to bear the expense of something that carries no strategic value, but that is just the nature of the business we are in. There is no exemption, unfortunately, from having to bear the expense of the onslaught of this intervention because by all rights we should get a pass as a demonstrably well-run organization for which best business practices, integrity, fairness in fact, and good taste have always been our guides to success. Almost before the ink has dried, our *dynamic* approach to this business has always allowed us to move forward, innovate, and respond flexibly in the service of our client customers, despite the increase in regulatory burden, cycle after cycle.

Value & Culture of our Bank

Values lead to *what* elements we consider & *how* we consider what actions to take.

Government = political way to change/organize human activity
Economy= financial way to change/organize human activity

CNB is a voluntary collaboration of its four constituencies (customers, colleagues, shareholders & community) which occurs everyday, supporting each of us individually and collectively, tangibly and intangibly, facilitating growth of the community.

"Human" equity is derived from the constructive interdependency of and among our four constituencies; this collaboration is the "secret of our sauce".

"Culture Eats Strategic Planning for Lunch"

The "Winningest" Model

Key Takeaways

- Mainstream and community banking is to commerce as oil lubricant is to the engine.
- Even though the banking business is perceived to be about numbers and ratios, two-thirds or more of the business is actually about the psychology of how people feel about the numbers.
- Growing the community fosters the bank's own growth and its increased financial strength that, full circle, promotes the growth of the community.
- Listen to markets and understand your organization's role and relevance to the people you serve, and design the strategic plan and mission goals so that you continue to add value and focus on building the customer relationships and free yourself to not get bogged down psychologically by compliance concerns. Regulation is incremental central planning (bad).

- Central planning (communism/socialism) is a failed economic system. Regulation is incremental central planning, best used sparingly when no other alternative is available.
- Human matters trump business affairs; relationships trump transactions!
- Government intervention to re-regulate is at best a *static* exercise, where we are a *dynamic* enterprise, constantly adjusting and adapting.
- Sales: we learn more by listening than by talking; learn the client's commitments and concerns.
- Compliance ultimate tool kit: Is it lawful, is it fair, and is it in good taste?

George W. Hamlin IV has been president and chief executive officer of The Canandaigua National Bank and Trust Company since 1979 and Canandaigua National Corporation since its inception in 1984. He is chairman of the Genesee Valley Trust Company and CNB Mortgage Company. Before joining the bank in 1978, he was associated with the Rochester law firm of Nixon, Hargrave, Devans and Doyle. He graduated from Yale University in 1963 with a BS degree in physics. He received his JD from the University of Virginia Law School in 1972.

Between college and law school, from 1963 to 1969, Mr. Hamlin served with the U.S. Air Force mostly throughout Southeast Asia as an F-105 fighter pilot accumulating 100 combat missions over North Viet Nam. Among his decorations are the Distinguished Flying Cross (DFC) and ten Air Medals.

A director of the newly formed New York State Wine & Culinary Center LLC, the informational and educational gateway to the New York State Wine Industry in affiliation with RIT and Wegman's, Mr. Hamlin is a director of C-MAC (Constellation Brands—Marvin Sands Performing Arts Center). He is a member of the board of the Center for Governmental Research Inc. and a member of its Finance and Investment Committee. Mr. Hamlin is chairman of the Investment Advisory Committee of the Monroe Fund, a venture capital fund underwriting expanding businesses in the Upstate metropolitan market.

Mr. Hamlin was elected to the Board of Directors of the Federal Reserve Bank of New York, where he served for six years (1997-2002), to include an unprecedented second term as the community bank member, and was chairman of its Audit Committee. He previously served on its Buffalo Branch Board for four years (1993-1996).

Mr. Hamlin is active in the activities of The New York Bankers Association (NYBA), is a current member of its Legislative Committee, and is a past chairman of NYBA, as well as of its Legislative Committee and its Trust Division. He is a past president of the Independent Bankers Association of New York State (IBANYS). He is a past member of the Government Relations Council of the American Bankers Association and is a Contact Banker for legislative matters.

Currently a director of the University of Rochester Medical Center (with which he has been associated since 1985), and chair of its Audit Committee, Mr. Hamlin currently serves on the Quality Assurance Subcommittee and is a past chairman of its Finance Committee. He is chairman (emeritus) and current member of the Board of Thompson Health System and each of its four operating subsidiaries.

Mr. Hamlin is chairman of the Board of Managers of the Eastman School of Music and a member of its National Council, and a Trustee of the Rochester Museum and Science Center, where he is a member of the Executive Committee and Finance Committee and chair of the Nominating Committee. In June 2006, Mr. Hamlin retired as a member for seventeen years of the acting company of the Bristol Valley Theater, a professional summer stock theater located in Naples, New York. He has been a commercial, instrument-rated pilot for well over four decades, is active in the development of the Canandaigua Airport, and, with his wife, is owner/operator of Canandaigua Aircraft LLC, which flies a Cessna 421C, Golden Eagle. He is active in many other professional and civic organizations.

Mr. Hamlin was inducted into the Rochester Business Hall of Fame, the first banker to be so honored, for innovation in the banking industry, inspired leadership, and commitment to the community. Also he has received a Greater Rochester Award for Board Leadership in the not-for-profit sector.

Mr. Hamlin and his wife, Mary, have three grown children—a daughter who is a family practice physician, a son who has a law practice in Canandaigua specializing in the defense bar, and a son who was graduated from the Eastman School of Music as a student of saxophone performance (double major: jazz, classical)—two granddaughters, and two grandsons.

Building the Organization, Serving Communities, and Developing Employees

Chris Van Gorder, FACHE
President and Chief Executive Officer
Scripps Health

ASPATORE

Introduction

I am the president and chief executive officer (CEO) of Scripps Health, an integrated tax-exempt health care system that includes four licensed hospitals on five separate campuses, and twenty specialty and primary care outpatient centers throughout San Diego County. We have a little more than 13,000 employees, around 2,600 integrated and independent physicians, and around 1,500 regular hospital volunteers.

Among health care leaders, I suppose I am somewhat unusual in that I have responsibility for our entire $2.3 billion operation, reporting to our Board of Trustees.

Situation-Dependent Management Strategies

Though I'm sure my management style has changed over the years, I have always considered myself a participatory manager, and I think that's still reflected in my role today—though it has become more situation-driven. There are times when my style needs to be directive, such as during disasters or crises. Our organization has responded to a number of local, national, and international disasters, for example, and a directive style fits these situations best.

Though a directive style allows me to move extraordinarily fast when necessary, my default, everyday style of management is participatory and collegial. This approach provides an opportunity to discuss issues meaningfully and reach consensus.

I have approximately seventeen direct reports with whom I meet weekly. Unless a direct report has a need to meet one-on-one, I usually meet with the group together so we can discuss the issues at hand and the organization's strategic direction. I believe all our senior leaders and all our managers are responsible for managing the *entire* organization, not just their components. So I expect my chief financial officer (CFO) not to concentrate only on finance issues, but also to understand organizational operations. If he truly understands the purpose and value of what we finance, he can leverage our resources more effectively. In the same vein, I expect our chief medical officer, head of strategic planning, and our general counsel to have an understanding of finance. As a result, we manage Scripps Health as a complete team—not as a group of individuals separately accountable only for what we know.

And, of course, there are a number of management style variations in-between. For example, I've learned over the years that a large part of my job is communicating and teaching—a more didactic approach. I've come to believe that one of leadership's most significant roles today is teaching, and that is particularly true in complex organizations going through significant change.

As health care reform measures begin to take hold in the next five to ten years, organizations like Scripps will definitely go through significant change. During this period of change management, I expect I'll need to call on a variety of management approaches to be successful. Right now, I'm a teacher, collaborator, and strategist as we begin to plan for a new health care era and prepare our employees and doctors for the significant changes ahead.

Process for Setting Goals

We formally update our strategic plan and long-term goals every three years and make adjustments annually. The formal process generally involves six months of planning, during which senior management and our Board of Trustees engage in a goal-setting process. The board regularly approves our annual and long-term goals and evaluates management and our overall success based on those goals.

Likewise, we have a formalized process for grouping our goals within five categories, such as Finance and Community Benefit. For example, using this method we establish thirty to forty formal goals that involve our workforce, physicians, and physician relations. All of these goals fall into our Community Benefit category because we obviously need physicians to do our work. Once primary goals have been approved by the board in each category, every layer of management, including frontline supervisors, drills further into those goals. All goals are computerized, tracked, and linked to the strategic plan, so it's a precisely aligned process.

Every month, the board reviews each committee's progress toward its goals. When the Human Resource and Compensation Committee meets, it reviews our workforce goals. When the Finance Committee and the Audit Committee meet, they review the financial and compliance goals, respectively. The whole process is dynamic and it happens monthly or quarterly, so we stay on top of things.

Working with the C-Level Team on Today's and Tomorrow's Priorities

I feel I enjoy close, personal relationships with my C-level executives. My entire senior executive team has been with me now for about nine years, and I've been here for ten. I came into the organization as the chief operating officer (COO) and was in that role for only about six months before I was elevated to the CEO position, when physicians across our system gave the sitting CEO a vote of no confidence. As part of my transition, I built a new senior leadership team that has been with me ever since. This means we know each other extraordinarily well professionally and personally. But they do realize, of course, that I am and need to be the boss. I am directly accountable to the Board of Trustees. However, our entire senior team sincerely supports me in that effort, so we all work closely together.

Although no one has left our leadership team, over the last couple of years we developed a succession planning system. Every year I formally prepare a confidential memorandum to the board that outlines my recommendations for a CEO replacement, should anything happen to me. The chairman and the board's Human Resource Committee each keep a copy.

And we have employed a more formal process when planning for other management team replacements. We literally create a six-foot wall graphic that lists *every manager in the organization.* The listings are color-coded in green, yellow, or red to indicate whether we have somebody ready to move into that position. For positions coded green, we have someone who is immediately ready and qualified. If we are training somebody to step in, we code that position yellow. But if a successor has not been identified, that position is coded red. Such a display gives our board and me a snapshot view of where we need to develop candidates for succession—and where we're in good shape with multiple candidates.

Role of Agility and Flexibility in Leadership Strategies

As I mentioned earlier, I came into this role upon the quick departure of a CEO who, for whatever reason, did not gain the confidence and trust of his medical staff and others. To this day, I think many of his concepts were sound, though his approach was what I would call too much, too soon. He believed that strategy implementation was a linear process: step one, step two, step three. If anybody objects, do it anyway to get to the next step. I don't believe strategy works that way at all. Strategy provides a useful guide, but to succeed, the leadership and implementation process still requires the board and management to continually re-evaluate goals, the marketplace, and organization readiness.

I'm not what you would call your typical health care executive. I'm an ex-cop who was injured in the line of duty. I spent a year as a patient, retired from the police department, and then the hospital hired me. A long time ago, I learned the police officer's secret for responding successfully to a call. The secret is to get there. You can't help anybody if you don't get there, and I believe the same thing about strategy and management. *The goal is to get there.* While you may not always get there first, you have to move your organization forward. So, just like a police car, you sometimes have to slow down and make a right or a left turn, and management and strategy are the same way. Sometimes you speed up the strategy. Sometimes you slow it down, and sometimes you change course by making a right or left turn. The intent is to keep the organization moving in the same general direction and to achieve your strategic goals. Consequently, you have to be flexible and agile, and I believe that is the secret for success.

Becoming an Employer of Choice

For Scripps Health, becoming an employer of choice became a specific goal about eight or nine years ago. We were losing money at the time, and our employees were, necessarily, concerned about the future of the organization.

As part of our turnaround process, one of my first acts as CEO was to rip up the strategic plan. I thought there truly was no reason to have a strategic plan when the doctors had only recently voted no confidence, our employees were angry with us, and we were losing money. I said, "We need to design an annual tactical plan right now that focuses on the things we absolutely must do to turn ourselves around so that we can survive until next year."

We first started working on relationships—specifically employee and doctor relationships. Then we focused on gaining financial stability and rebuilding the balance sheet. Then, over time, we started striving for what I think is the top of the pyramid for health care—*quality*. However, quality improvements can be expensive, and they can't be accomplished without the engagement of your physicians and staff.

We knew we needed to evaluate the areas that were adversely affecting our employee relations, so we went to the Great Place to Work Institute—the organization *Fortune* magazine uses to determine its national list of top employers. We surveyed ourselves across the board and kept the survey comments anonymous. We provided incentives for our employees to participate in the survey and assured them they could be and needed to be candid. As a result, we attained between 95 percent and 100 percent participation and, on a scale of 0-100, scored 55 the first time out. National best practice at that time was in the high 80s. This was a terrible score, but the survey gave us specific data on which areas were troubling employees. And that year we received 700 pages of written comments in response to the following two questions:

1. What makes us a great place to work?
2. What would make us a better place to work?

I'll admit some of the comments were hard to read, but I read every single one, and from this information, we designed a series of incremental goals that began with the things that our employees needed the most.

We have since repeated this process every year. We still enjoy a high level of survey participation, but this year we scored 89, which puts us in the top-100 category of employers. Today I get 2,000 pages of comments. Most of them are much more positive than they used to be, and together they provide the context for our entire employee relations goal-setting process. Scripps Health is now considered a destination workplace and a top national employer, and it all began with listening to our employees, getting objective data, setting reachable annual goals, and then building on those goals.

Developing Employees for Future Roles

Earlier I touched on succession planning at the management level and ensuring we're regularly developing new leaders. Similarly, Scripps had no system for generally developing employees. Moreover, the hospitals operated as separate entities—in complete silos. Because we didn't operate as a system, we didn't even have a management or employee education program. It wasn't long before our head of human resources (HR) developed a division we call the Scripps Center for Learning and Innovation. We hired educators, developed training programs for our managers and others, and began coordinating education throughout the entire system. That program now includes training and education at every level of the organization, including orientation for new managers, a dynamic and growing emerging leaders program, and an employee mentorship program.

Perhaps a lynchpin in our employee development is our Scripps Leadership Academy, now in its tenth year. Leadership Academy is a year-long program that annually accepts twenty-five to thirty manager- and leadership-level "students." In full-day, monthly, facilitated sessions, we expose classes to different topic experts from inside the organization and discuss roles, responsibility, management style, career growth, business strategies, operational decision-making, and much more.

The Leadership Academy arguably provides the most in-depth orientation to how things *actually* work within our organization. I personally participate in every monthly session, beginning with more than two hours of open questions and answers (Q&A). If participants don't ask tough questions, I provoke them. All topics are on the table except individual personnel issues and the contents of confidentiality agreements. Transparency is incredibly important to this process and to our success as an organization, so we want those involved in the academy to understand how the place truly operates, why managers do the things they do, and the processes we go through when making decisions.

Graduates from the academy have since formed an alumni association, which manages and drives our quarterly system-wide, all-management meetings. Additionally, the Academy Alumni initiated and operates our Hope Fund, an employees-helping-employees program for employees needing financial assistance. And they manage some of our bigger operational and cultural events, like our annual Quality Summit. Overall, Leadership Academy graduates serve as an advisory group for me. And, as a further investment in their development, we recommend and finance five to ten graduates each year for a two-year health care operations fellowship program with the Advisory Board in Washington, D.C.

The whole purpose of our employee development program is to change the culture of the organization from silos to system, and we've experienced amazing success. Together, these programs offer a comprehensive approach to developing employees. While management always likes to have a loyal group of employees, I rarely see corporations and businesses show loyalty in return. I believe loyalty should extend in both directions. If we are going to sustain a strong culture at Scripps, we have to commit to the people who work here. While we'll always also look outside for the best possible job candidates, I truly believe in developing and promoting people from within and giving them new opportunities.

And I believe this commitment should extend to a philosophy of "no layoffs." Though this is never something a CEO can promise, it's a general philosophy that goes toward mutual loyalty. While nothing stays static, and every organization must continue to redesign itself and tweak operations here and there, our Scripps Center for Learning and Innovation also operates our Career Development Services Program. When good business dictates changes that eliminate jobs, those affected employees enter the Career Development Services Program at full pay, where we retrain them, update their résumés, and put them in the lead for other jobs that open within the Scripps' system. Over the last five years, we've found that 80 percent to 90 percent of employees going into the program take another job within the system, while about 10 percent decide to leave the organization on their own. Even when the economy soured, Scripps did not resort to layoffs. To us, this philosophy is a community obligation and an organizational imperative.

Best Practices for Communicating Effectively

In our organization, we communicate every way we can, and it's those many conversations that lead to success. To begin with, every employee in the organization has direct access to my e-mail address and, thus, direct access to me. I take this open-door policy seriously and respond to every e-mail I receive. To develop a connection with our staff from the beginning, I also speak often at our weekly new employee orientations and at every new supervisor orientation. In these sessions, I learn more about who is coming aboard at Scripps, and who is taking on a leadership role. And I'm able to share my expectations of how they should perform and how they will uphold our number-one goal: for our front line staff, that's taking care of patients. For our supervisors and managers, it's taking care of our employees, so they can take care of patients.

This commitment to communications also extends to crises. If we happened to have an earthquake here today, we would immediately start polling all of our campuses for status updates and quickly get that information out to all staff. We also take great care in providing outside information and news to our staff in crises. If our staff can feel secure knowing they're regularly updated on what's happening within Scripps and near their homes, they can securely focus on patient care and feel comfortable working during what can be personally frightening events. We never want them to feel alone.

Of course, we also communicate internally through the usual channels: print publications, intranet, face-to-face forums or town halls, e-mails, focus groups, and more. And I speak at many different events and subgroups— accepting every invitation from a manager that I'm able to accept. Our marketing-communications department includes people assigned to each of our locations responsible for local communication and branding and for assuring system-wide communications are appropriately delivered. Additionally, our quarterly system-wide all-management meetings directly reach more than 600 managers with information, education, and discussion on changing policies, procedures, and strategies. Finally, we're moving now to more interactive communication techniques, testing the effectiveness of internal video available online and various internal social media approaches.

Delivering to the Community

As a community-based, tax-exempt organization, we have a responsibility to give back. We deliver just shy of $300 million per year in benefit to the community, either through direct charity care or through the care of people for which we receive no—or insufficient—reimbursement. We also provide prevention education in the community to help people better care for and prevent illnesses, such as diabetes. There is an epidemic of diabetes and type II diabetes in America today, and we're trying to prevent the spread and impact through better education, information, and health care access. Our community classes range from those that are disease-specific to classes on nutrition and general health—necessary components of a healthy life and disease prevention.

In addition, our community benefits include:

- Operating three highly regarded graduate medical education programs that provide nursing, physician, and general clinical training
- Medical and health research, including our translational science research program that works to move new research discoveries quickly from the research bench to the patient bedside
- Wireless medicine research program—working with wireless companies throughout San Diego and the United States to develop and suitably test new wireless health care products
- Operations of two of San Diego's six designated trauma centers, a level-I and a level II center. This includes training of U.S. Navy physicians in trauma prior to deployment to war zones overseas.
- Grants to organizations in our community that need financial support for health-related projects

Staying Abreast of Trends

I believe that continuing education is essential to keeping up with new health care trends. I serve as the chairman of the 39,000-member American College of Healthcare Executives (ACHE), which believes that a leader's obligation includes continuing education.

I receive formal education through ACHE and other programs across the country, as well as read constantly. Literally every morning, the first thing I do is check local and national newspapers and media outlets to learn about news and recent trends in health care. Then I copy any relevant article and send it out to my entire senior leadership team, our Leadership Academy alumni, our Physician Business Leader Cabinet, and our Physician Leadership Cabinet.

All of these people then know what I'm reading, and hopefully they're sharing the information with their people, so we can keep everyone focused on the changes happening in health care. Then, of course, we'll apply that information to our goals and strategies and make adjustments accordingly.

Lessons Learned

You have to trust your leadership team, and you must focus on accountability. In health care especially, we honestly don't know what will affect us next year. We don't know whether the federal government will trim our Medicare reimbursements or whether the State of California will trim our Medicaid reimbursements. We don't know whether we will have a big flu season (which will increase the numbers of our hospital patients).

So, while we create budgets and plans based on historical norms, they can vary quite dramatically. I'll never forget watching people (who, in some cases, I learned from) tell the board during a year when they performed poorly, *"Well, who could have expected this?"* And the board would nod and say *"OK. Well, let's hope we do better next year."* Well, the bottom line is that we're supposed to predict changes in the marketplace, build contingency plans, and adjust quickly when things occur that we have not predicted. In other words, we're expected to be accountable for the business operations, just as a patient who comes to the hospital expects us to be accountable for his or her quality of care. I don't tolerate excuses for failure to perform, and I don't accept them in myself, either.

When talking to our new supervisors, I always draw a triangle on the board and ask, *"When you looked at your job description, what were you looking for?"* And generally, I find that they have considered two sides of the triangle: their responsibility and their authority. They may even ask for more responsibility and authority. However, in all my years in management, nobody has ever asked me for more of that third side of the triangle, which is accountability. Nobody ever comes in and says, "Chris, I want more responsibility and authority, and I expect you to hold me more accountable." By nature, I guess, most people don't want to be held accountable. I always tell people, "To me, the definition of accountability is that if you miss your targets once, you won't be here to miss them twice." Now, that sounds very strict, and it is—however, I've never terminated anybody based on this philosophy. I've found that when you make the rules of the road explicitly clear, and people completely understand what they're accountable for and the consequences they'll face for not performing, they will perform.

Like almost everyone, I've also found that managers don't like to make tough decisions. They put them off until they absolutely have to make them. Yet, who pays the price? At the end of the day, our patients and employees pay the price for management's failure to make decisions in a timely manner. After nine years of pushing this rule of accountability, we've regularly hit our financial and quality targets, and we've been a member of *Fortune* magazine's "Best 100 Companies to Work For" from 2008 to 2010.

I truly believe our success is based on management's understanding that they are accountable for achieving established levels of performance. Because excuses are not tolerated, they remain focused on what they *need to do* every day and not just on what they *want to do* every day. I truly believe that if people understand the rules of the road and the expectations, they will perform. They won't let you down.

Key Takeaways

- One of leadership's most significant roles now is to teach, particularly in complex organizations that are going through significant change.
- All managers are responsible for leading the entire organization, not just their components.
- Sometimes you need to speed up the strategy. Sometimes you need to slow it down. Sometimes you change course by making a right

or left turn. The intent is to keep the organization moving in the same general direction and to achieve your strategic goals.

- When you make the rules of the road explicitly clear, and people understand what they're accountable for and the consequences they'll face for not performing, they'll perform and won't let you down.

President and chief executive officer (CEO) of Scripps Health since 2000, Chris Van Gorder, FACHE has led the not-for-profit health system through a remarkable financial and cultural turnaround, and in the process has positioned Scripps among the nation's leading health care institutions.

In addition to his duties with Scripps, Van Gorder serves as chairman of the American College of Healthcare Executives (ACHE). As chairman, he provides leadership for an established network of more than eighty ACHE chapters that provide local access to networking, education, and career development. ACHE is also known for its prestigious FACHE credential, signifying board certification in health care management.

Mr. Van Gorder oversees all functions of Scripps Health, which operates five acute-care hospital campuses, nineteen outpatient centers, and regional home health care services with more than 2,500 affiliated physicians and 13,000 employees.

When Mr. Van Gorder was suddenly named CEO shortly after arriving at Scripps in 1999, Scripps was in trouble. It was losing $15 million a year; its medical staffs had voted no confidence in management; and employee morale had hit bottom. Mr. Van Gorder responded to the crisis with a direct and steady approach.

Having completed a $125 million turnaround, Scripps is now at the beginning of a $2 billion growth and expansion plan across the region. Its workforce is also thriving, as Scripps was named to Fortune magazine's list of "100 Best Companies to Work For" in America in 2008, 2009, and 2010.

Mr. Van Gorder's rise to health care executive has been unconventional. His journey began as a hospital patient, when as a police officer he was critically injured during a family dispute call. After a lengthy recovery and starting a new career in hospital security, he continued his education in health care management and rose to levels of increased responsibility.

Mr. Van Gorder continues to serve the public today as a reserve commander in the San Diego County Sheriff's Department Search & Rescue Unit and as a licensed emergency medical technician (EMT). His volunteer work was honored in 2006 with the Maltese Cross Award: Spirit of Courage by the San Diego County Fire Chiefs, and again in 2007 with the MedAssets Outstanding Humanitarian Award. He was recognized in 2008 with the inaugural Ronald H. Kendrick Regional Stewardship Award from LEAD San Diego. And in 2009, he received the distinguished B'nai B'rith National Healthcare Leader Award.

As an instructor for the Red Cross, Mr. Van Gorder also certifies Scripps employees in CPR, first aid, and emergency response. In 2008, the Red Cross recognized him as Real Hero for saving the life of a community member using CPR.

Mr. Van Gorder received his master's degree in public administration and health services administration at the University of Southern California, completed the Wharton CEO Program at the University of Pennsylvania, and earned his bachelor's degree from California State University, Los Angeles.

In March 2006, California Governor Arnold Schwarzenegger appointed Mr. Van Gorder to the California Commission on Emergency Medical Services, and in 2010 Mr. Van Gorder was reappointed. In January 2007, U.S. Secretary of State Condoleezza Rice reappointed him to the U.S. Commission for the United Nations Educational, Scientific and Cultural Organization (UNESCO). He currently serves on the board of directors of the San Diego Regional Economic Development Corp. He is a clinical professor in health administration at the University of Southern California, where he also serves on the Board of Councilors of the university's school of policy, planning, and development. In 2007, Mr. Van Gorder received USC's prestigious Guardian Award for his significant achievements in health care and his commitment to the community. And in 2008 he received the Learning for Life Distinguished Citizen Award from San Diego—Imperial Council's Learning for Life and Exploring Division, an affiliate of the Boy Scouts of America.

In 2007, 2008, and 2009, Mr. Van Gorder was named one of the nation's "100 Most Powerful in Health Care" by Modern Healthcare magazine, and in 2008, he and his executive team were named the Top Leadership Team in Health Care for large health systems by HealthLeaders magazine. In addition, Mr. Van Gorder is a member of the editorial boards of HealthLeaders and the Governance Institute.

Mr. Van Gorder was part of medical history following Hurricane Katrina in 2005, when U.S. Surgeon General Richard Carmona, MD, asked a Scripps medical unit to staff a temporary clinic for hurricane survivors in the Houston Convention Center. The request for Scripps' assistance marked the first time the federal government asked a private health care organization for long-term support for a nationally organized disaster relief plan. Most recently, Mr. Van Gorder traveled to Haiti with the Scripps Medical Response Team to aid victims of the devastating earthquake that struck on January 12, 2010.

Leadership through Tumultuous Change

Virginia A. Barnes
President and Chief Executive Officer
United Space Alliance LLC

ASPATORE

Introduction

The U.S. space program is in turmoil. The space shuttle program is scheduled to conclude flights in 2011. The president canceled the largest space development program (Constellation) to return humans to the moon. Commercial space operators are emerging as potentially viable providers. The International Space Station (ISS) has been targeted for use through 2020. The United States will have to depend on Russia for sending its astronauts to the ISS. For the first time in fifty years, the United States will not dominate the world in human space flight capability.

United Space Alliance (USA) follows the U.S. space program. USA has successfully operated the space shuttle since 1996, including astronaut training and provisions, refurbishment of the shuttle components, and mission operations. On a much smaller scale, USA participated in the Constellation program and the ISS program. USA houses the only organic human space flight capability outside the National Aeronautics and Space Administration (NASA). The gap in space flight operations created by this turmoil causes USA to redefine its strategy and to seek alternative markets for its unique capabilities.

As the president and chief executive officer (CEO), I am responsible for the successful transition of United Space Alliance from the NASA primary space shuttle contractor to a much smaller, more competitive supplier to NASA and a variety of other customers. USA employment, once over 10,000, is currently around 8,000 and expected to be around 3,000 to 4,000 within the next year. Annual revenue of $2 billion is expected to shrink by 60 percent to 75 percent over the next twelve to eighteen months. USA success on the space shuttle program as the exclusive provider of support and services must translate into success on a much smaller scale and within a highly competitive landscape. Unique capabilities developed to support the space shuttle program must find application in other markets with a variety of customers.

Headquartered in Houston, Texas, USA was established in 1995 as a limited liability company; USA is equally owned by The Boeing Company and Lockheed Martin Corporation and has 8,100 employees working at sites in Texas, Florida, and Alabama.

The business has been thriving since its inception. As the shuttle program ends within the next year, USA faces immense challenges in transforming to a smaller, differently focused company over the next twelve to twenty-four months.

I am new to my position, having assumed it in April 2010. Prior to joining USA, I spent twenty-nine years at The Boeing Company working on myriad defense and space programs. Knowing little about USA and given the fate of the space shuttle program, I was quite concerned about the member companies' expectations for the future of USA. I talked to the member companies' advisors and attended one board meeting. Was the members' intent to continue or dissolve United Space Alliance, especially with the shuttle program going away? Both member companies assured me that they saw USA as a crown jewel in their portfolios and as a national asset to NASA. With those assurances, I was comfortable accepting this position. USA intends to capitalize on that outlook, especially with the workforce declining significantly as the shuttle is retired.

Implications of Reducing the Workforce

NASA extended the shuttle program into fiscal year 2011, with the last flight scheduled for February 2011 and the potential of another flight in June 2011. Each additional flight extends the workforce, which means a stronger base longer, but it also presents some challenges. In parallel with safely flying the shuttles, we are establishing the foundation of the company and its future long-term structure. We are developing the strategy to market our skills to new applications with new customers. We are committed to developing the appropriate business model for the company post-shuttle. We are aligning the organization structure and the salary and benefits to accommodate a more competitive rate and overall cost structure. Rather than having a clean break from the shuttle program, we are starting on our new, post-shuttle path while still operating the remaining flights. Many of our resources work on both. About half of the employee population will be laid off post-shuttle.

The company has been doing a great job over the last two to three years preparing employees for the end of the shuttle program. The most important element has been communication of the program status and the implication to the work force. USA has communicated program and employment status to each employee. USA has provided critical skills bonuses and attractive severance packages to employees. In addition, USA has provided outplacement services, training and certification, and financial planning resources to employees at risk of losing their jobs. USA leadership has lobbied its member companies and other industries to find jobs for employees. Employees across the board recognize and appreciate the USA efforts to place employees. In fact, the companies assisting with employee outplacement have praised USA for its proactive efforts in employee preparation and placement.

Even though the employment changes have been communicated well, reality is now setting in. There was a layoff event in October 2009, but most of those leaving were self-nominations. In June, we had another layoff event, again mostly self-nominations. We had a layoff of about 1,400 people in October 2010. Of this last large group, fewer than 20 percent were self-nominations. This is an important difference for USA; the company had selected few employees to be laid off, but this time it had to do so by a significant magnitude. Remaining employees are intensely focused on the safe shuttle operations through the phase-out of the shuttle. Nonetheless, employees are saying farewell to long-term friends whom they view as family members and wondering how long they will stay employed.

Since joining the company, I have done some studying of the previous USA CEOs. The member companies appoint the CEO, the chief operating officer (COO), and the chief financial officer (CFO), and it appears that this company has enjoyed the right kind of leadership at the right time.

For example, when USA was first formed, Kent Black came in as an honest broker from Rockwell International. He was trusted by NASA customers and considered a visionary, someone who could successfully bring two primary, disparate organizations together. My predecessor was Dick Covey, former astronaut and space icon. He successfully carried USA through a contentious strike three years ago. He also began the shuttle transition roadmap to develop and communicate the plan of the company as it transitions. Preceding him was Mike McCulley, also an astronaut and well regarded throughout this industry. He led the company through the Columbia accident and return to flight of the space shuttle. McCulley succeeded Russ Turner, the longest-term CEO, who grew USA in the industry. Every USA CEO has been the right person for the company at the right time. My résumé fits the needs of USA right now with my business and program management experience, and my experience with this NASA customer and Department of Defense (DoD) customers.

USA's business has been primarily with NASA. We will expand that to a variety of customers, including the DoD, as well as subcontracting to our member companies. We have been a prime contractor with primarily a single large contract, but now we will be a much smaller company with a broader set of customers and many smaller contracts. While we've enjoyed an exclusive environment, we will now have to compete on our home front (sometimes against our member companies) and on new fronts.

Leadership and Goals

I describe my leadership style as communicative, inclusive, and team-oriented. It has been effective so far in setting a new direction and goals for our company. We formally set our goals annually, making changes as needed. During that process, we establish our plan for the five-year horizon. I have been reviewing the transition roadmap that Dick Covey established to identify areas for enhancement or change and to validate our current direction. My review, assisted by industry experts, has confirmed that we are heading in the right direction, and we have not missed any important areas.

Our ongoing programs have been highly successful, involving mainly the shuttle program, whose goals are jointly established via contract with NASA.

Our company goal-setting process will likely become more frequent over the next two years as we mature, as the political climate changes, and as NASA develops its plans for the future human space flight programs. The direction of NASA depends on politics. The outcome of those political debates could determine in large part what kind of future USA has, particularly if the next major program has a prominent role for our critical skills. That would define a solid direction for us. The timing of these decisions is critical. Although a decision today would not avoid upcoming layoffs, a near-term decision could still protect critical skills for human space flight and other related space operations work.

The Obama administration rolled out a NASA budget that was not well received by the Congress, and now Congress has come back with its appropriations proposals. Congress has been working with the White House to reach an appropriate NASA budget, which appears to be somewhere between the program of record—the Constellation program—and President Obama's plan, which delays the deep-space capability for five years and relies on commercial providers to transport goods to the space station.

Employee Development

Developing employees is also a large part of my job as CEO. One of my early mentors told me that the more you grow in an organization, the more your job is to find the next "you" and bring that person along to succeed you; that is more important than anything else you do. Mentoring has since been a key part of my job.

At USA I have established a few mentoring relationships so far, particularly for the purpose of helping some of our executives who will no longer be employed after the shuttle leaves to find their next jobs. I am doing everything from critiquing résumés to talking about interviews and helping with decisions on what might be the next best path—anything to help find the next right opportunities for them.

In the current environment, it is important for USA to identify and retain the right skills. While the overall focus is downsizing, convincing people to stay is a challenge. For those with enough fortitude, I believe the opportunities will be great, once we survive the end of the shuttle program and the definition of the NASA direction.

Communications

We have a strong communications organization that takes care of all the external and internal communications for our organization, and they do a terrific job. As for me, I tend to be as transparent as possible, and I tell people what I know. If I cannot tell them, then I tell them that I cannot tell them. Even in times of uncertainty, it seems that if you tell people you do not know the answer, it is better than not telling them anything because you maintain your credibility.

I also publish what I call Ginger Grams, a name that an employee engagement team coined based on my nickname years ago, for my informal but mass communications to the team. I sent one out recently letting people know that we were not the successful bidder on a contract we were going after. Even though NASA awarded the contract to another company, our proposal team did an excellent job, and I wanted to recognize them for the work they had done. I also wanted people to know we will work with NASA to understand what drove their decision and will continue to aggressively seek new business. Ginger Grams can be about any subject; they are essentially a mechanism for me to get communications out rapidly.

We have also used a variety of other means to communicate. We recently used a Webcast to reach all the employees at one time, rather than having an all-hands meeting at twenty different locations. That approach worked well, judging by the feedback. We also have brown bag sessions and roundtable discussions with smaller audiences and a more intimate setting—lunches, breakfasts, and other similar venues, depending on what we want to communicate.

Recognition

Another important facet of my job is motivating the workforce, which we do in several ways. We have an internal recognition program called Quest for Excellence, where people are recognized quarterly for performance in several parameters including safety, leadership, quality, technical, administrative, and community service. We participate with NASA in the space flight awareness program, where employees are recognized for special contributions. The employee and a guest go to Kennedy Space Center, where they are given VIP treatment for a launch, as well as special tours and memorabilia.

NASA astronauts also recognize the value of employees, and they award Silver Snoopy to deserving employees. USA employees train the astronauts, clothe the astronauts, pack the bags for the astronauts, and are the last ones to button them into the shuttle. Thus, our employees know the astronauts extremely well. The astronauts themselves developed the Silver Snoopy award, and it is a high honor. I am proud to say we have a large number of Silver Snoopy recipients in the company.

We recently established an enterprise-wide employee engagement effort. In my experience, when you have the employees engaged, that means they take responsibility for their actions. They feel an ownership in the company. Leadership releases reins and lets employees highlight ideas, concerns, and recommendations. It can be useful for everything from facilities problems that you would never think about to layoffs to how we recognize employees and their stellar careers as they are laid off. So far, we have employees engaged in pockets, but I want to do it across the board. Through all the challenges we currently face, company leadership must understand the challenges of the employees. Tapping into this key resource will help us focus our strategy and maintain two-way communication throughout the company.

Meeting Expectations

Reinforcing accountability within the company is essential to performance. I tell people my expectations and how they are doing against those expectations.

We establish certain performance factors or criteria annually. We rate employees' performance against those criteria as part of their annual performance reviews and any incentive opportunities.

This company has been wildly successful since its inception, and it continues to outperform its targets. It is hard for us to make changes when we have been so successful, yet recognizing the need for change, communicating that change, and getting people aligned with that change are all necessary—and challenging. We need to become flexible and agile, especially as we go from a single-contract company to a multi-contract company. We must be able to meet a variety of customers' needs, get to know the customers, and apply our capabilities to their needs.

As CEO, I have four primary values. The first is people. People are our key resource, and if we take care of them, they will take care of us. The next one is passion. We have to have a passion for what we do to be as effective as we can be. That is not hard to do in the space business because it is so exciting; it is interesting work; it is challenging work; and it is historic in many cases. The third one is promises. Promises made should be promises kept, and that gets back to the expectations. Promises we make to the customer are a commitment, and we stand by that commitment; we fulfill it or beat the plan. Performance is the final value; that is foundational to everything we do and we must always seek to continuously improve our performance.

Lessons Learned

In my role, something different crosses my desk every single day. One day it may be a technical concern; the next day it may be a new benefits plan. The variety is exciting, though sometimes daunting. I am largely responsible for 8,000 people.

Being the CEO of this company is a never-ending stream of challenges. I am fortunate in that I inherited a talented and courageous team. I learned as much as I could when I entered the position and have a great network of trusted resources to tap into. If I were to offer advice to upcoming executives, it would be to have a network of mentors—not just one. Have mentors for everything, every different thing you might encounter. Have a mentor for people issues. Have a mentor for fiscal issues. You might even have someone you can call on when you have a technical issue. You always want to have a host of people who will serve as resources for you.

Key Takeaways

- One of my early mentors told me that the more you grow in an organization, the more you need to find the next "you" and bring that person along. Developing and mentoring employees is more important than anything else you can do.
- Be as transparent as possible, and tell people what you know. Even in times of uncertainty, telling people you do not know the answer is better than not telling them anything at all.

- When employees are engaged, they take responsibility for their actions and feel ownership in the company. Let go of some of the reins, and let your employees tell you what they want, rather than what you think they want.

- I have four primary values: people, passion, promises, and performance. People are your key resource, and if you take care of them, they will take care of you. Second, you must have a passion for what you do to be as effective as you can be. Third, promises made are promises kept. Finally, performance is foundational to everything and can always be improved.

- Build a network of mentors for everything so that you always have a host of people to serve as a wealth of resources you can call on for any given issue.

Virginia A. (Ginger) Barnes is president and chief executive officer (CEO) of United Space Alliance LLC. As president and CEO, she is responsible for the direction, development, and operations of the company.

Barnes joined USA as president and CEO after serving as vice president, chief operating officer, and deputy program manager for The Boeing Company's Brigade Combat Team Modernization Program, formerly the Future Combat Systems Program. In addition to overall program execution, Ms. Barnes's responsibilities in that role included program financials, customer interface, human resources, strategic staffing, LEAN, and employee engagement.

From 2006 to 2008, Ms. Barnes was vice president of weapons programs and the St. Charles site leader for The Boeing Company. She led the integration of direct attack programs (JDAM, Small Diameter Bomb) with surface warfare (Harpoon, SLAM-ER) missiles.

From 2004 to 2006, Ms. Barnes was vice president of Naval Support Systems, where she was responsible for all sustainment solutions for Navy and Marine Corps customers. She developed this customer-facing organization consolidating all logistics functions and programs to include performance-based logistics programs (current and proposed), depot partnering, and field service representation.

Preceding that position, Ms. Barnes was the director for business management of the F/A-18 Program. Appointed to that position in May 2002, she had responsibility for providing a focal point for all services related to business management for the F/A-18 Program. Prior to that, she was the director of contracts and pricing in aerospace support. She also served as deputy business manager.

From 1993 to 2000, Barnes held numerous roles of increasing responsibility and complexity with The Boeing Company, having joined Boeing in 1981 in Huntsville, Alabama, as a financial cost analyst. She then served as program engineer, contracts administrator, contracts manager and international contracts manager for a variety of programs.

Ms. Barnes graduated with high honors in accounting from The University of Alabama at Huntsville and earned her master's degree in business from the Owen Graduate School of Management at Vanderbilt University. She is a commercial pilot and instructor and has served as an FAA-designated examiner for hot air balloons.

Dedication: *I dedicate this chapter to my many mentors, including Margaret Greer, Doug Stone, Scott Carson, Bob Ingersoll, Jim Albaugh, Pat Finneran, Brewster Shaw, and Dick Covey. Special dedication goes to my dear husband and biggest champion, Toby Barnes.*

Leadership:
Some Successful Strategies

G. Mark Armour

Senior Managing Director and Head, Invesco Institutional

Invesco

ASPATORE

Introduction

Leadership comes in many forms, from the most obvious, such as president of a country or chief executive officer (CEO) of a major corporation to the less obvious, such as leader in your family or among your friendship group. So most of us have had more leadership experience than we often realize and probably took on our first leadership roles quite early in our lives. As the eldest of four children, I know I did. As well, leadership is something some of us deliberately seek, while others have it thrust upon them. Either way, having a defined leadership approach or set of leadership strategies will help in making you more effective. While the strategies briefly set out in this chapter are specifically focused on leadership in a business environment, most will be applicable in more general leadership roles.

The strategies set forth here are based on some thirty years' experience in leadership roles in the asset management industry, as well as broader leadership roles, such as chairman of an independent girls school and a director of a number of publicly listed companies. I've lived and worked in Australia, Hong Kong, and the United States, and many of my roles have been global in nature, so this discussion reflects my experiences with a range of different cultures.

My current role is senior managing director and head of Invesco's institutional business. Invesco is an independent, specialist global investment management firm operating in twenty countries and providing services to institutional and retail clients globally. We are publicly listed (NYSE, ticker, IVZ), with total assets under management of some $580 billion (August 2010). I am responsible for a number of key parts of the business. These include four large investment centers—Invesco Fixed Income, Invesco Real Estate, Invesco Global Strategies, and Invesco Private Capital, including WL Ross & Co. These groups manage some $275 billion for clients globally across a wide range of asset classes, from cash and traditional fixed income to global and quantitative equities, asset allocation, and alternatives, such as structured products, property, and private equity. My other responsibilities include U.S. institutional sales and service, coordination of our global institutional sales and consulting relations activities, global performance and risk, Atlantic Trust (our high net worth business) and the chairmanship of the Invesco Product Committee.

I have been in my current position for four years. My role has changed significantly in that time, as it often does when assuming new responsibilities. During the first year, I was much more focused on troubleshooting, fixing immediate problems, and being reactive in nature. Today, I manage much more proactively with a longer-term focus. The initial imperatives were getting the structure correct, putting strong people into key roles, and strengthening our investment capabilities. Today, with those key elements in a good place, the emphasis is now on achieving strong organic growth.

We viewed the difficult economic and financial environment of 2008 and 2009 as a threat, yes, but frankly more as an opportunity to differentiate ourselves from our competitors. We were cautious over 2007 and especially going into 2008, so we were careful not to over-extend ourselves. We maintained a strong focus on our core business of investment management and stayed close to our clients. We also used the time as an opportunity to speed up the implementation of our strategic priorities. The difficult circumstances made it easier to make tough decisions, which we did. This approach served us well, as we are generally regarded as one of the better performers in our industry over the last few years.

Leadership Style

The words I would use to describe my leadership style are "adaptable, open and direct, and outcomes-focused." My key areas of focus are ensuring clarity of vision and strategic direction, setting the bar high, creating a strong culture of client focus, integrity, and trust, working hard to get the best people, and over-communicating. I emphasize fact-based decision making, which is applied in a fair, consistent, and transparent manner. As much as possible, I try to remain calm on the outside and work hard to do the right thing, recognizing that as leaders we must also make the difficult decisions. And it is all about outcomes. As I often say, "Talk is cheap—money buys the whiskey!" Finally, let us not forget that as leaders, we spend the majority of our time fixing problems—some major, many trivial, but all important.

Leaders must be adaptable, as I don't believe there is any one management style that works best in all situations. I've lived and worked in Australia,

Hong Kong, and the United States, and the experiences were quite different from each other. As a leader, you need to be prepared to adapt your management style to your circumstances, which can include the country and culture, the group of people you're managing, and the challenges and opportunities facing the company, as well as the economic environment. There may be times when you need to use a more old-style command-and-control approach, but more often than not, you want to be inclusive, flexible, and more of a confidant and a colleague than a boss.

Setting the Direction

It is obviously important to clearly establish your vision, strategic objectives, and business priorities. As part of your vision, you should think about setting big, aspirational targets. It is important as leaders that we set the bar high in terms of our goals. What do you want to achieve, and realistically, how much can you achieve?

Determining your priorities also means deciding what you are not going to do. A mistake that many leaders make, particularly when we are younger and inexperienced, is that we try to do too much. Being realistic about what you can achieve means making conscious decisions about the issues you are not going to tackle today. You must stay focused on your key priorities and work hard not to be distracted by the myriad of small and less important matters.

Finding the right balance between being tactical versus strategic is also important. Your broad, strategic direction should not change. What will change, however, is the magnitude of your focus on certain areas, which will depend on various factors, such as industry conditions, market conditions, and the evolution of the firm. Agility comes into play in how you tactically translate your strategic focus and where you apply that extra effort.

Company Culture

An area that is extremely important for Invesco and that I believe is critical for any leader is an emphasis on organizational values and, in particular, integrity. One of the most important things a leader must do is communicate a clear set of values widely within the organization. Putting them down on a piece of paper is the easy part, but it is meaningless if not supported by actions. Leaders must "walk the talk." What leaders do is much more important than what they say, and staff are extremely observant of your actions when you are in a leadership role. Therefore, the behaviors you exhibit as a leader of your organization are critical in determining the behaviors for the entire organization.

Then, you need to make sure you get buy-in; it is important to talk to the employees and discover any cultural issues early so that you can address them. Critically, as an asset manager, we have a fiduciary responsibility on behalf of our clients, so our values and our integrity must be more than just words on a page.

A strong shared culture is a critical precondition for success in any organization. However, it takes time to establish. If you're in a firm that is undergoing change or some sort of evolution, it is important to recognize that it will take time for the culture to become embedded all the way through the firm. You may be able to align the senior managers relatively quickly, but then you need to work with them to communicate and align the rest of the organization. Second, your company culture must be about actions, not just words. Culturally, we want people to understand and operate consistently with the firm's values.

So, what are these values we want shared throughout the organization? For us, some of these key values are a focus on clients, integrity, trust, and the recognition that working together we achieve more. We need people who want to do the right thing and who are capable of doing the right thing for our clients, for our staff, and for our shareholders. Balance is important—if we're doing something that is good for one group at the exclusion of the other two, then it probably isn't the right thing to be doing.

The leader's actions, particularly with respect to decision-making, will shape the firm's values. It is critical that you are seen to make fact-based decisions that are made after wide consultation and applied consistently throughout the organization. You must strongly resist showing any personal favoritism and must never indulge in personal criticism of team members or allow such personal comments to be made within the team. These actions will strongly support the values of integrity, trust, and working together.

Just as you set a high bar with respect to business goals, you must also set a high standard for acceptable personal behaviors. This means setting the tone from the top, but then being quick to address any examples of poor personal behavior you become aware of within your organization. A failure to address bad behavior, especially by your senior team, will be seen as tacit approval of their actions and therefore will quickly undermine other efforts you're making to improve behavior in a manner consistent with the company's culture.

Culture and values have become increasingly important to me over the years. The senior leadership, more generally, and I, specifically, focus tremendous effort on ensuring we employ only people with a strong value set and who we believe are strongly culturally aligned with our values.

Talent Management

It is important to surround yourself with the best people you can find, get them bought in to your vision and strategy, and then let them get on with their jobs. I do not believe in micro-management. As implementation and execution are much more important than strategy, I place a strong emphasis on employing people with a demonstrated track record of success and a strong value set. In hiring the right people, if you find you're a good judge of character, trust those instincts. I believe in hiring from within, but I'm also comfortable with making key hires from outside the organization when it makes sense for the business. Having a clear vision that you can communicate to the potential candidates makes it much easier to find the talent you want. People want to be part of something successful, so articulating the opportunity, the vision, and the success helps you hire the talent you want.

I look for a number of other key attributes in the people I work with. I like them to be intelligent and passionate about their jobs. They should be comfortable making decisions and want the accountability that comes with doing so. Nonetheless, they should look to push down decisions to increase accountability throughout the organization. Their decision-making process will be fact-based and will be the result of wide consultation with relevant colleagues. I also prefer working with people whose egos are under control and who have a tendency to under-promise and over-deliver.

People are our key resource in asset management, as they will be in most businesses. Therefore, it is important for us to have a strong employee value proposition to ensure our staff are motivated, successful, and engaged. At an individual level, we have a formal annual performance review process that starts with goal-setting and includes six-month and annual reviews. But managers should talk with their key people regularly, and the contents of a performance review should never be a surprise to the staff member.

Separate from the annual performance review, we also have an annual talent review process where we identify those in the organization who have exceptional potential. While most staff will have some form of agreed-on development program, for this group we have a more comprehensive and individually customized approach. A key element of development is on-the-job training. Accordingly, our annual talent management process culminates in an all-day meeting of the Invesco senior group (CEO plus nine senior managing directors), where we discuss the high-potential group and agree on future development roles for them.

It's important, as well, to gauge how employees feel about the business and their comprehension of the firm's strategic direction. We conduct a staff survey of all employees every eighteen to twenty-four months. We use an external firm to ensure confidentiality and to give us external benchmarks. The survey assesses a wide range of factors, including understanding of our strategy and direction, assessment of senior and business unit leadership, understanding of values, etc. Ultimately, though, it is an assessment of how engaged our staff are with Invesco. From this survey we can monitor progress period to period, as well as measure our standing against external peer groups, such as our industry sector, or most importantly, global high-performing firms.

We obviously look at other metrics, such as staff turnover and so on, but the staff survey is a critical input for us to make sure that our people management is actually translating into improved staff engagement and satisfaction. Reflecting our efforts, our staff survey results have improved considerably over the last four years, so that as a firm we now rank ahead of the financial services norm and in line with the norm of high-performing companies.

Communication

As a leader, you must over-communicate your vision, strategic priorities, values, and progress. You can never communicate these too much. For a global firm like ours, we have many audiences: we have shareholders, a range of clients from institutional to individual retail, and the staff. Therefore, we need to make sure we use the right communication vehicles for each audience, taking into consideration geographic locations, cultures, and languages. We need to make sure we're using multiple avenues, such as simple written communications, e-mail, other Internet sources, conference calls, Webcasts, face-to-face meetings, and so on.

Given this wide range of audiences, consistency of messaging and repetition are paramount. Your saying something once does not mean you can assume that people will remember it; rather, you need to make sure there is a strong consistency to your messaging over time. Be simple, clear, and concise, and evolve your messages slowly over time so that all audiences know exactly what you're saying. You have to repeat things so that your staff and your clients clearly understand your message and recognize you mean it. If you keep changing that message, it will be difficult to achieve buy-in. Finally, your messaging needs to be delivered at multiple levels so that the cascade of messages reinforces the ideas set forth from the top.

There is a second type of communication, namely internal, within and between teams. The majority of the issues we grapple with as leaders and managers ultimately come back to a lack of communication. Accordingly, it is important to consistently emphasize the need for people to talk with each other. Problems will nearly always be resolved by discussion. Remember face-to-face communication is more effective than by telephone, which in turn is much more effective than e-mail. E-mail is obviously important to us all, but does not take the place of direct face-to-face interaction.

Continuous Learning

Experience is the most valuable learning you can have. Accordingly, take advantage of any leadership opportunities you are offered, both inside and outside of work. Second, observe closely the leaders you work with—particularly those who are viewed as most effective. Work at observing leaders in different walks of life. There are many lessons to be learned from capable leaders in politics, sports, culture, etc. The challenges we face as leaders are continuously evolving. Therefore, as good leaders, we need to look to learn something new every day and seek to constantly improve ourselves. We all have a management style that we are probably most comfortable with, but you need to recognize the importance of adaptability, and to instill that adaptability in all our employees, as well.

Finally, it does make a difference that you are in a job you enjoy. You will likely be more successful if you are passionate about your role and your position.

Key Takeaways

- As a leader, be prepared to adapt your leadership style according to current circumstances.
- Clearly establish your vision, strategic objectives, and business priorities. Set the bar high.
- Culture and values are critically important. I emphasize client focus, integrity, trust, and working together.
- Leaders must walk the talk. What we do as leaders is more important than what we say.
- Decisions must be fact-based and consistently applied.
- Spend a great deal of time attracting, nurturing, and motivating excellent people.
- When communicating, keep messages simple, clear, and concise. Repeat often.
- A good leader learns by experience and by observation and strives to improve continuously.
- Do what you love and make sure your passion comes through.

G. Mark Armour is senior managing director and head of Invesco's Worldwide Institutional business, positions he has held since January 2007. He is responsible for four main investment groups covering traditional and alternative capabilities, managing more than $200 billion, as well as sales, service, product development, and performance and risk activities.

Previously, Mr. Armour held senior leadership roles in the funds management business in Australia and Hong Kong within Invesco, AXA and ANZ.

Mr. Armour is a director of the NYSE-listed Invesco Mortgage Capital and a trustee of the Georgia Council for Economic Education.

Mr. Armour received a bachelor of economics (with honors) from La Trobe University in Melbourne, Australia.

Moving Past the Status Quo to Excellence

Stephen F. Ronstrom

President and Chief Executive Officer,
Western Wisconsin Division

Hospital Sisters Health System

ASPATORE

Introduction

I am president of the Western Wisconsin Division of the Hospital Sisters Health System (HSHS). There are five divisions within HSHS, which operates around the world. Thirteen HSHS locations exist in the United States and are in Wisconsin and Illinois. Our corporate headquarters is in Springfield, Illinois. As Western Wisconsin Division president, I report to the chief operations officer (COO) for the system, who reports to the Sisters and the governing executive board.

My responsibilities as president of my division include planning and carrying out the provision of our health care services to a population of about 450,000 people. What is unique about us is that we provide health care in partnership with large medical groups, as well as independent private practice physicians in the Upper Midwest. We work in cooperation with them, and although the partnership aspect can be challenging, we have been successful. We have excellent outcome statistics—in fact, we have some of the best in the country.

Changing Roles and Responsibilities

Our health system has shifted away from its inpatient focus in recent years, so on a personal level, much has changed for me, as well. I have evolved from a project management role to chief executive officer (CEO) of an institution, and then to CEO in a division of the health system.

During my tenure as CEO of a HSHS institution, I led the development of two five-year strategic plans to build harmony in the medical community and secure a joint agreement with an area clinic. My priority was to minimize excess operating costs and reengineer management services to provide a patient-focused system. Under my leadership, the hospital gained a patient satisfaction rating in the top one percent in the nation, as measured by Press Ganey, and received three "Top Performer" awards and four "5 Star" awards for physician satisfaction.

As CEO of a division of HSHS, we have had many successes—due in large part to the stellar teams at our hospitals. We have added robotic surgery with the daVinci surgical robot and executed a $40 million upgrade to our

Imaging Services area. A major undertaking, our Smart ORs (operating rooms) added an intraoperative MRI to a neurosurgical suite and an intraoperative CT to a spine/trauma surgical suite.

Keeping the pulse on outpatient services, we have adjusted our processes to ensure we remain fiscally viable. Our leadership and colleagues participate in a cross-hospital surgery task force to address opportunities for increasing quality and efficiencies. Needing to build a new emergency department, one of our hospitals raised $4.1 million in six months—a huge accomplishment that underscores the level of physician, colleague, and community support for our hospital.

As a result, I have had to learn to work with and through others to get the job done. I have also become more accustomed to planning further out in the timeline with a greater focus on resource allocation. The key lesson I've taken away is recognizing the importance of the people I work with—hiring the correct people for the job is critical.

A Happy Workforce

While we enforce a stringent, high-performing structure at HSHS, we also realize how important it is to create a happy workforce. A joyful or happy workforce has been a deliberate core value for our organization. We know that the way we treat and relate to one another is the way we will treat and relate to those we serve.

We are committed to empowering people to find meaning and value in their lives. We want people to feel that they are contributing to the greater good and working in an area that provides the greatest meaning in their life, and we will do what we can to assist them in developing a career plan so that they can discover what brings them the greatest personal reward.

I strongly believe we run a good shop when it comes to human resource policy and practices, but our real driving force is the way we develop leaders and train our employees. Our approach to employee happiness is unique in this industry. Most people focus on the customer more than on the employee, but we need to honestly and sincerely empower our employees properly and help create meaning in their lives, while also making sure the work systems are logical.

We are always focused on developing our talent. Our board of directors is involved in the succession planning process, and we have a thorough talent management assessment to find staff members who can grow with our mission. Essentially, our succession plan works by allowing our A-team executives to mentor other upcoming A-team employees. We have a formal place for each key executive so that if one leaves, we have someone we can move into the position who will do an excellent job. We also seek new talent outside the organization when we want to reinvigorate the division.

Communication Strategies

Communication is a critical success factor for every executive. In our organization, we utilize a structured, but full, communication strategy and system. It is important to have clarity, vision, purpose, and a proper system in place. It is also important to understand that working with other people is essentially a communications issue. Our communication strategy goes back to our core value of compassion; if we are going to be compassionate, we have to be able to connect with others.

We take our leaders off-site for two days every quarter and immerse them in strategy and execution. During that time, we have informal interactions where we try to remove barriers and encourage them to deepen their relationships with each other and feel comfortable working with one another.

Equally important is hiring people who care and then empowering them so that you create a team effort to achieve goals. We have a real commitment to a healing presence, so our nurses, clinicians, and colleagues listen and connect emotionally and spiritually. Listening is part of the healing process. Because listening skills cannot be faked, we hire those who honestly care about others. For us, listening is not just an ability. It is an actual mindset.

We take advantage of new tools and practices to help improve our communications. In our case, we use actual scripts we provide to people to cover various situations. For instance, as we roll out new programs, disseminate strategic information, or reach out to key groups in our community, we provide all leaders with speaking points to ensure our messages are consistent and that we are "speaking with one voice."

Because of our efforts, everyone can work together without political infighting, and our focus can be on our mission. We also focus on getting the required work done because we have formed the intention early to connect with other human beings and to make sure their needs are met.

Finally, it is important to us that we keep everyone constantly informed. We use television sets around the institutes to run updates, the latest thank-you notes, and the news of various successes. We also keep people informed through our intranet, newsletters, structured department monthly meeting agendas, and division-wide e-mails. As previously mentioned, we use our off-site sessions to embed what needs to be communicated, and we place a real emphasis on what is most important—our mission.

Responsible Leadership

Part of our organizational responsibility includes our commitment to the community and the environment, which is built into our strategy, action planning, budget, and operational improvements. I like to be involved in these projects and make it a priority to bring the outside in to take part in these initiatives on as many levels as possible.

We participate in national endeavors, including various environmental and sustainability practices. For example, our food service director went to Washington to address the U.S. Department of Agriculture (USDA), which has drawn national focus. He spoke about the success of our partnerships with local farmers and institutions in bringing healthful, organic food from the farm to our patients, staff, and members of our community. Ten percent of a $2 million food budget at one of our institutions is dedicated to the purchase of locally grown and produced fresh food. That institution has received the national Practice Greenhealth Environmental Leadership Award two years in a row and has enabled other organizations to follow its buy-local lead by helping create and launch a local Producers & Buyers Co-op.

We expect anyone who steps into a supervisory or management position to be involved in the community, and we make it part of his or her career development plan. We expect leaders to partner with the community groups and leverage the hospital's resources. For instance, we serve meals to our patients in the hospital, and we do Meals On Wheels for the elderly in our community who cannot leave their homes.

A top priority for us right now is quality. Health care and business costs being what they are today, we have to train and structure innovation in all of our practices. We expect our employees to continually seek performance improvements on an individual level.

We also have a major commitment to technology, as evidenced by our recent installation of a MEDITECH system. I believe that innovation and technology are the basics for addressing our social issues going forward. I am convinced that we must train our staff, set our standards and practices, and ensure that we are implementing medical technologies in the same manner we are aggressively implementing quality measures in our institutions.

Our efforts in these areas have not gone unnoticed. We recently won the Wisconsin Forward award, and we will continue striving for improvement. That means hiring smart people and asking enough of them to keep them on top of their game. We will always be looking at doing things better. We need to create a climate where we all take ownership for the way we do our work and how we can improve it.

Creative Approaches

Creative approaches to problem solving, such as our recent installation of a MEDITECH system, have contributed to our success. Several other big and small examples stick out in my mind, the first being the new Smart Operating Suites in our Brain & Spine Institute. These two suites include a configuration of imaging and mapping technology so sophisticated we needed to obtain special state regulations for wiring. Leading neurosurgeons perform some of the world's most complex brain, spine, and trauma surgeries using the technology in these operating suites. In fact, only six hospitals in the world have two operating suites like these. The result has been a significantly higher-quality outcome for those patients treated in the new suites.

At HSHS, we decided not to wait for federal efforts on health reform and launched a movement we are calling Imagining the Future: 2016. Usually community health needs is a boring topic; you go to the public health department and get the latest statistics on who died from what and who has communicable diseases and so on, but we are taking a new and creative approach. We started a movement here to connect with our community, asking them to imagine and help us create the ultimate in health care for them, their families, and the community. We started the conversation and have found that people's requests were not unrealistic by any means. In truth, they wanted fair pricing; they didn't want to sit for an hour-and-a-half waiting for the doctor to see them; and they were interested in wellness initiatives. By engaging people in the community on these issues, we are creating stronger relationships and beginning to truly understand our patients' needs.

We run on a lean budget, but lack of funds does not deter innovation. For instance, we recently adopted a new practice in nursing care that is simple, but yields great results. Instead of a nurse giving her hand-off report to colleagues in the nurses' station at shift change, that nurse can report out to the next nurse in the patient's room. The nurses go from room to room together, with one reporting and the other listening. This method saves time and affords the patients the opportunity to comment on or update the nurses' reports, as well as giving the patients the additional comfort of knowing how their needs are being met.

I recently presented to our board of directors an example of another creative approach our staff initiated. Our lab department decided to reroute everything, so they emptied the lab room of its equipment and replaced it in a manner that made better sense for them—cutting the number of people walking back and forth in circles and creating a logical flow. The result is that we were able to reduce errors and improve lab results response time. The approach that the laboratory staff took made sense: it allowed the actual users to redesign the room to their specifications, as opposed to an architect or process engineer.

In summary, there is plenty we can do with lean practices and training our employees to always be looking for ways to improve the process.

A Philosophy of Leadership

It is important to keep in mind, however, that even when people say they are ready for a change, you need to be ready to articulate clearly the impact of those changes. If people are going to be significantly affected, you need to take the time to communicate and talk them through the process. While they may not agree with you, they will at least understand the reason for these changes.

Moving past the status quo to excellence can be a lonely journey. While change may make sense to your employees, be prepared to face some resistance. It is human nature.

We need to view one another in partnership. Every organization has its politics, and to learn how to operate in partnership with others can be a challenge. We all need clear training on managing commitments and expectations.

Gauging Success

At HSHS, we have a formal system of feedback involving our performance review, direct one-on-one meetings, and monthly progress reviews to evaluate how we are doing. We work toward developing a relationship of trust, mutual respect, and solidarity. I find the best feedback comes directly from my staff. I appreciate their transparency and honesty in alerting me to difficulties.

We also use computer-generated anonymous feedback, as well as coaches. I take advice from a group of people outside the hospital; I like to think of them as my external personal board of directors.

In addition, I make a point of reviewing each day as it ends. I walk through my day just as Ben Franklin did and ask myself whether I could have handled situations better. Questions I ask include: Do I need to go back tomorrow and make amends? Do I need to confront this person? Is there something more going on here that I need to be aware of? I go through that process each day as part of my own self-awareness and as a way to connect to my higher power and get feedback.

Key Takeaways

- Do not underestimate the importance of a happy workforce. The way we treat each other and relate to one another is the way we will treat and relate to those whom we serve.

- Communication is a critical success factor for every executive. Equally important is hiring people who care and then empowering them.

- Moving past the status quo to excellence can be a lonely journey. While change may make sense to your employees, be prepared to face some resistance. It is human nature.

- Always seek both formal and informal feedback to keep a pulse on the organization and determine whether adjustments need to be made.

Stephen F. Ronstrom, MHA, serves as president and chief executive officer (CEO), Hospital Sisters Health System (HSHS) Division (Western Wisconsin). He was appointed administrator of Sacred Heart Hospital in Eau Claire, Wisconsin, in 1998. Today, he leads the regional HSHS mission through Sacred Heart Hospital and St. Joseph's Hospital in Chippewa Falls, Wisconsin.

Combining health care business expertise and management with social service, Mr. Ronstrom led Wisconsin hospitals in 2008 by pledging 10 percent of Sacred Heart's $2 million food budget to purchasing local food from family farms. Under his leadership, Sacred Heart received prestigious honors, including the Practice Greenhealth Environmental Leadership Award for innovations in environmentally responsible health care and the 2009 Governor's Forward Award of Excellence, the highest achievement level possible under the Wisconsin Forward Award. He was also personally honored with the Catholic Charities "In My Name" award, presented in 2008 by La Crosse Diocese Bishop Jerome Listecki for contributions to the social mission of the Church.

A pioneer in accessibility, Sacred Heart Hospital, under Mr. Ronstrom's leadership, is the only health care provider in the community to have always provided care for patients covered

149

by BadgerCare (Wisconsin's program for the uninsured) and continues today as the largest provider in the region.

Mr. Ronstrom is a fellow of the American College of Healthcare Executives and has served on local boards, including the United Way, the Economic Coalition, Catholic Charities, and the Chamber of Commerce. He currently serves on the board of the Wisconsin Hospital Association.

Listen to the Music: A Look at Successful Leadership Strategies

Bruce T. Mulhearn

Chairman and President

Prudential California Realty

ASPATORE

Listen to the Music behind the Words

My wife Tomazina and I are the sole stockholders in our entities: Mulhearn Realtors, also known as Prudential California Realty, the Mulhearn Group, and Castlehead Escrow. We have been in business since 1967 and have twenty offices with more than 800 agents. I am involved in most aspects of management, mainly through delegation. Accountability is achieved through our key executives, and we set strategy for the company primarily involving growth. Acting as a public ambassador for the company, my role is also being a motivator and morale builder.

Our business model is different from most in the real estate industry. Management is selected at both corporate and branch office levels. Agents are all independent contractors. We have eleven staff members at our corporate office. Our general manager is located at one of our training centers and is in constant communication with each of our branch office managers. There is an open pipeline to the branch office managers through our general manager.

Through key agents in each of our offices, I invest time, breakfasts, lunches, and telephone calls to receive feedback to determine what the business and political situation is in each of the branches—they are my sounding boards. It is vital to keep a finger on the pulse. We also have joint venture offices, where my corporation normally has a 50 percent interest in the office profits and in turn provides all the support systems—recruitment, training, marketing, accounting, and technology. The joint venture owner is involved in the day-to-day management of his branch office or can delegate that responsibility to a third party. The profits are split: 25 percent to the individual manager of the branch and the remaining 75 percent split 37.5 percent going to the joint venture owner and 37.5 percent going to my corporation.

Our business model does not include a board of directors. There is an advisory board of some key executives, and we just have informal meetings. Sometimes we meet one-on-one, depending on the issue we are discussing, and healthy debates are part of our process. It is often said that the best committee consists of three—two who are absent. I don't necessarily agree.

The Evolution of the CEO and the Company

Looking back on my first attempt to manage an office, it began with one part-time agent and quickly grew to nine agents. We expanded from 600 square feet of office space to 1,200. The doctor next door moved offices so we were able to expand our space to accommodate the nine agents.

One of our agents decided to quit, even though we were the most productive company in the city. He indicated that as I was a selling manager, I did not have time to train him—to invest valuable mentoring so he could improve. At first I blamed him; we normally point the finger in directions other than at ourselves. He was told how I brought in large amounts of business with listings he could use, and I did not take floor time, which led to incoming business as a great benefit to him, but he did not buy my argument. That evening I had a mental wrestling match and asked myself whether I wanted to be a selling manager in the field for the rest of my life or build this company through proper administration.

The decision was to change my method of operation, so I turned over the vast majority of my buyer and seller leads to my sales force, wondering whether I had made a mistake. In most cases, I had not. I then had time to create a formal training program, teach it, bring in an able assistant to delegate responsibility, and set up affiliate companies in both escrow and mortgage. For the first six months, I watched production decline with some serious losses because my personal transactions were no longer on the blackboard. However, during that same period, we went from nine to twenty agents and found ourselves with the sales back on the board, and I was not participating in them: one step back, two steps forward.

We then had another setback. As we grew, we obtained an additional 1,200 square feet of space in the small free-standing building behind us. A competitor across the street who was influential with the city council had our curbs painted red all around my office. My agents did not have anywhere to park. That incident forced me to buy our first commercial building within a mile of where we were conducting business. We bought 16,000 square feet, slowly removed the existing tenants, and filled the building with agents as our business grew.

The next leadership challenge that came was to open our first branch office. I learned a valuable lesson—the best sales people do not necessarily make the best managers. One of my top agents threatened to leave unless I gave him the opportunity of managing a branch office. At the tender age of twenty-six, I was more of a risk-taker than I am today, and so he managed a new office branch thirty minutes away from our original office.

That was my biggest mistake.

Hindsight indicated I should have opened an office within five to ten minutes so my sales force could be equally divided without anyone leaving the direct marketing area in which we functioned. We could have continued to advertise in the same newspapers, which was more important in those days, and training would have not been difficult, as we would have been closer together. By moving thirty minutes away, those opportunities were lost; it was a totally different marketplace. We had no identification there for expansion.

We chose a small three-bedroom, two-bath house in a commercial zone—another mistake. After eight tedious and expensive months, we closed the office with a loss of approximately $25,000—a huge amount of capital in the '60s. The next time we opened an office, it was closer to our original one; we did not have to divide the sales force the same way; I did not have to offer higher commission splits for agents moving away; nor did I have the additional challenge of the remaining sales force wanting a raise in commission split, too.

Defining moments in every CEO's life determine the future; we endeavor not to have history repeat itself. I have been through five business recessions. The first was in 1964, when the savings and loans in California ran out of capital. We accomplished whatever was necessary to create financing and have transactions close.

In 1974, the next recession, during President Carter's tenure, when gasoline was rationed and there were lines of cars waiting for fuel on odd and even days, affected the whole marketplace.

In 1979, I had 500 agents, twenty offices, and $1.7 million in the bank. In 1982, I had six offices, 125 salespeople, and $300,000 in the bank. This was a perilous period, when interest rates climbed to 18 percent, but we survived. Because of that experience, we changed the model of our company—golden handcuffs would be the answer. Our model now comprises joint venture offices with fellow owners working for profits.

In 1990, the Berlin Wall came down, and our peace dividend in California was the loss of 500,000 high-paying jobs in the aerospace and defense industry, along with the loss of 300,000 support jobs. The loss of jobs had the effect of reduced property values creating home foreclosures and major vacancies, which reduced transactions. Making payroll in a tough market can be a daunting proposition and a humbling experience.

The real estate industry is cyclical by nature; it is constantly changing. We learn to adjust to change and adapt to the marketplace to survive. Prior to the last three years of recession in California, we had four real estate schools and were hiring up to 700 primarily new agents per year. Our emphasis was on beginning training so that the agent could go through the transition period and evolve into being a competent agent. However, in the past three recessionary years, the majority of our effort has been recruiting experienced agents, which is more difficult, as many are settled into their existing companies.

Another major change is we have centralized our recruitment department; this has become a top priority and to some degree the highest and best use of my time. It is important to endeavor to meet a candidate and spend a minimum of fifteen to twenty minutes in a presentation directly with him. By providing that valuable time, I am demonstrating that I am not in an ivory tower. The almost unique portion of our program is the use of company capital to assist our agents and sellers in creating transactions. The seller has the benefit of bridge and cosmetic repair loans, which expedite transactions and maximize return for the seller. We also have joint ventures with our agents where we purchase property—the company provides all the capital, does charge points and interest for it off the top, and the agent and the company each receive 50 percent of the profits. It is a great recruitment and retention tool.

Setting Goals Using SMOST

We have cultivated several goal-setting philosophies over the years. One is the use of the acronym SMOST, consisting of the following:

S: Situation analysis: my present position

M: Mission: the mission statement for the company; a simple paragraph of the overall vision for the company

O: Objective: ongoing priorities with no timelines

S: Strategies: the long-term response to a particular challenge

T: Tactics: the short-term, day-to-day functions to accomplish that strategy

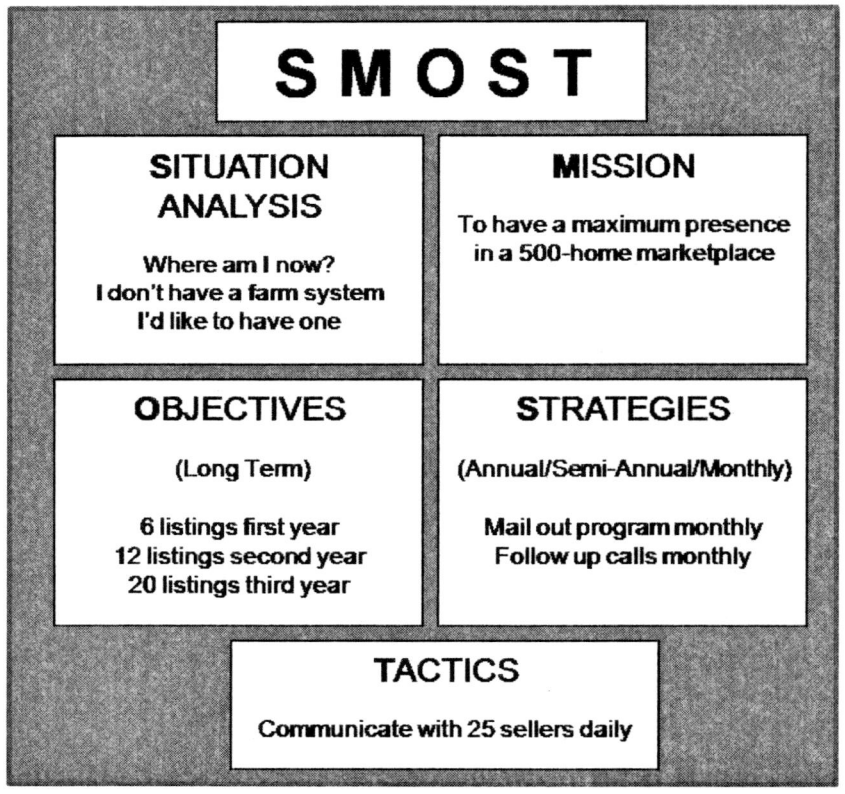

In addition, I categorize the ten activities I like best outside of family and business. And I constantly review the six major areas of my life: family, financial, mental, physical, spiritual, and social. Once I complete those exercises to identify the goals, they are reduced to writing and prioritized. One needs to continually examine goals to modify them based on changing internal and external conditions. For instance, an interest rate change might necessitate a marketing campaign. The priorities in a recession are different from those in an up market. In addition, as we grow older, some of our goals need to change. At one time, I was a marathon runner. Now I use an elliptical machine instead because my knees have taken a beating over the years. Be flexible. Allowing yourself to change goals can become highly productive. Communicating my goals gives guidance to my fellow team members and agents, but in the final analysis, it's up to them how they handle advice.

Development, Training, and Keeping a Happy Workforce

To motivate our sales force, I do the best I can to think outside the cliché box. I review Maslow's hierarchy of needs and recognize that each person is different. Some want monetary incentives; others enjoy having the use of our company limo for awards ceremonies and recognition. We attend formal and sometimes informal dinners and have access to condominiums we use as gifts for holidays and getaways.

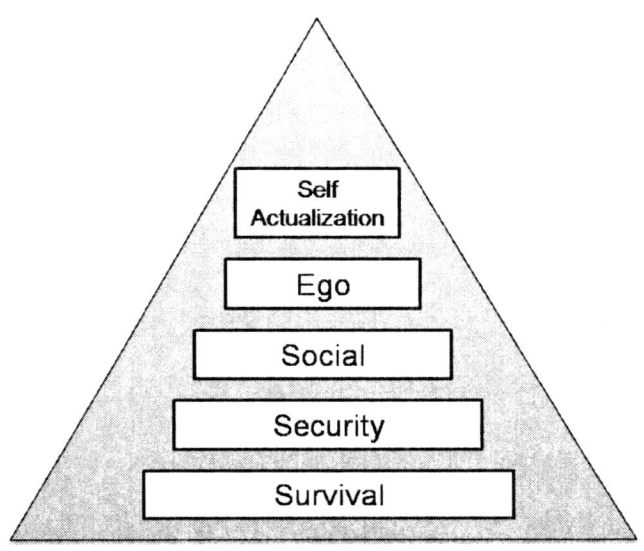

MASLOW'S HIERARCHY OF NEEDS

For the top twenty-five agents, annual awards at the Ritz Carlton are special. Learn to surprise people with the unexpected—an award of a three-day trip to a destination resort, a meal at their favorite restaurant with or without my wife and me coming along. Do not suggest Italian food if their preference is Chinese. While I do not send Christmas cards, every employee and agent receives a birthday card; birthday cards are more intimate and have a better message.

Training in every level is critical, and I have a passion for teaching so we focus on developing agents at all levels in our organization. In the real estate industry there is a designation named the Graduate Realtors Institute, which I co-wrote and on which I taught the first course in 1970 in San Diego. On the national level, there is the Realtors National Marketing Institute, for which I participated in the writing of the Certified Residential Specialist course, which I taught in Miami and Seattle to get it off the ground. As a senior instructor, I taught the Certified Residential Broker course for fourteen years.

In earlier times, I tried to save everyone in our company by providing these various training opportunities—a task I now conclude wasted a tremendous amount of time and effort. Over the years, I have come to the conclusion that an agent has to have a combination of courage, high energy, self-discipline, and a sense of urgency. Also, I now recognize in training sessions that the goal of education is not knowledge, but action. If there's no action, then we suggest the agent have a career adjustment. It becomes important to ask continually whether someone is worth the effort and then follow through.

On another topic involving intensity, a close friend once told me to keep a piece of paper in my pocket on which I had scribbled, "He could be right." My friend suggested I pull it out from time to time to read it when I am involved in a serious discussion with someone who has a difference of opinion. I love the expression, "Good judgment comes with experience, but experience comes from bad judgment."

Frequent personal contact with the most important and successful agents in each of our branches is critical. I communicate in person if possible, but time constraints typically have me using the telephone, and even then, it is sometimes impossible to reach out to everyone. When in-person or telephone communications are not viable, the next best bet is to use e-mail, fax, Facebook, or our weekly marketing e-mail newsletter. Also, I frequently deliver to my managers and agents CDs and DVDs to illustrate points I need to make.

In personal presentations I give to agents coming in from other companies or the business, I explain that while this is not rocket science, at the risk of being repetitive, we do need courage, high energy, self-discipline, and a sense of urgency. These qualities apply to a CEO as much as anyone else. In our business, I emphasize a thousand details can be compromised by one or two missing parts.

All agents in the company have the voluntary opportunity to attend my Advanced Training Program. It takes place every Thursday morning from 7:30 to 9:30. For that program, we bring in selected top agents from various parts of the company to conduct a program for thirty minutes on a topical of interest. We record this portion of the session, and those in attendance receive a copy of the CD the following week to reinforce the learning experience from the prior week. At these advanced training meetings, I give out three or four books to read by pulling agents' cards from a hat. A number of regulars give short reports on the highlights of the week before, and we summarize and discuss them briefly. It is never mandatory to attend, and our agents come and go; some gain success in our business while others fail.

Maximizing the performance of the workforce is always an uphill battle. We have advanced training weekly also for management. We have an eight-week course for a full day on Saturdays for people transitioning into our business, as most of them have regular Monday through Friday jobs before they come on board. We have commercial training to teach people to complete a 1031 Exchange (a kind of tax-deferred transaction), and to sell an apartment building, commercial building, shopping center, or small industrial complex. We have quarterly award breakfast meetings, where we bring in top speakers from around the country and normally have half of our sales force show up for such an event; nothing is mandatory in our company because our agents are independent contractors.

Hearing the Music: Mentoring and Succession Planning

Mentoring strategies and day-to-day tactics are the responsibility of our branch office managers. We do have job descriptions for mentors, but leave it to the managers to delegate and carry out the function; in some cases the manager acts as the mentor, while in others he gives the responsibility to someone else.

In the beginning, as a manager in a mentor role, I was more inclined to be a star, rather than a star-builder by mistakenly wanting to do the work on the salesperson's behalf instead of showing him how to do it. It took a great deal more patience to allow the salesperson to try as I watched; after all, I was egotistical enough to believe only I knew how to do it correctly. I sat there gritting my teeth, wanting to jump in. By not jumping in, I was allowing him to be the one to succeed or fail. If he failed, then I could step in and hopefully save the transaction. Did we lose a few transactions by taking a chance in choosing this method? Yes, but in the long run, it taught the salesperson how to fish. In catching a fish for him, it would feed him for a day, but leave him hungry the next. By teaching him to fish, it allowed him to feed himself for a lifetime. A good manager has to not only learn what someone is saying, but hear the music behind the words or the body language that coincides with the words.

The best example of hearing this music came from a long-time friend, Howard Brinton, a national real estate trainer. One Sunday Howard called on an old high school buddy to play a game of golf. When his friend took the call, he was in the kitchen with his wife who was preparing an early dinner for her parents. The husband placed his hand over the receiver and said, "Howard's in town for one day. He wants to play a round of golf, OK?" His wife protested, "But my parents are coming over for dinner this afternoon." The husband persisted and responded, "But it's Howard, my best friend." She then replied, "Then go ahead and enjoy yourself." Those were the words, but in the tone of her voice, the music indicated that if Howard did not stay for dinner, then the locks on the door would be changed. On many occasions, the words spoken are only a small percentage of the true message being conveyed. It is the tone of voice, the delivery of the words, and the body language that accompanies what is said that are vastly more important.

Succession planning in our organization has been an area of neglect. I would fail at retirement, and I foolishly believe I will live forever. My oldest son is heavily involved in our business and would be the obvious replacement. He and I understand that he will need to continue to adapt to that particular position by being involved at the corporate culture level, as he now runs a branch office. It will require balance between his personal beliefs and those practices that have worked for me. We need to remind ourselves, "If it ain't broke, don't fix it."

Creating and Defining Company Culture and Vision

Part of our vision, mission, and values has always been to remain in an expansion mode, with the objective of increasing the size of our company every year. Sometimes exterior conditions prevent this from happening, but in the past three years of recession, we have either merged with or acquired five separate offices. Three out of the five are making profits. We expect within the next year-and-a-half to two years, they will all be in that position. Our actual mission is not complicated; it is to have customers and clients for life. Our vision is to behave in such a way as to make that occur, and success will depend on our values coinciding with the Realtors Code of Ethics.

The Prudential name has given us a different cultural style and has upgraded our image. I am no longer concerned about relegating the name Mulhearn to the Prudential name. At first, I do confess that it was an ego enema for me. Whatever works is what we want, and we believe the Prudential logo works better than Mulhearn. As another cultural plus, I have a pool of capital available for the offices and agents to facilitate successful closings using short-term swing loans, bridge loans, and cosmetic repair loans, cash for keys, and the agent enrichment program, which enables agents to purchase real estate by using company capital. We do have the constant marketing of the Prudential brand through print media, websites, social media, platform, and consumer direct. We also provide major press releases for weekly newspapers spotlighting our more productive agents. These are then reprinted and delivered to them for their spheres of influence.

It is difficult to have a consistent culture with the variety of personalities in branch office management. As previously mentioned, we have improved the culture of our company by becoming a Prudential regional franchisee. We pay royalty dues to Prudential National, with part to Warren Buffet, who owns the franchise in California. To be associated with a national brand such as Prudential, which has been around for 135 years, gives us added credibility, particularly in a new marketplace—that is why I chose that particular brand. In the old pre-franchise days, we had to spend hundreds of thousands of dollars to earn name recognition, and now that is no longer necessary. We also have the added advantage of Prudential being a financial services company, so in a sense we are receiving a partial free ride on their advertising.

Our business model is based on joint-venture compromise and some individual autonomy. With joint-venture owners in our offices, I cannot persuade the same way I could if I had sole discretion in our company. As branch office joint-venture owners, they do have more say in regard to decisions. The major benefit of this model is that each of us has a vested interest in controlling expenses. When a dollar goes out for telephone, advertising, or anything else, my joint-venture owner is as involved in that process as I am because, like me, he wants to save capital. Company culture also stems from both managers' and agents' perception of me as the role model; I am usually in the office by 7:15 a.m. unless I have a meeting and normally work until 6:30 p.m.

Reinforcing Accountability through Role Modeling

One way we reinforce accountability in our organization is to release a list of our top twenty-five agents monthly and the top fifty annually. We broadcast these results to the balance of the company as role models. We publish the top ten most productive branch offices each month and send out what the gross commission income is for the first one or two to give others a target to shoot for.

We are constantly looking at different methods to improve our offices and are now finding that having co-managers in some cases is advantageous. Management consists of visibility and availability four hours a day for each co-manager and the balance of time to be used for personal productivity. It seems to be working well, and it gives our management team much more freedom. For additional accountability of our management team, we have an outside coach who holds telephone conferences with groups of four managers per session weekly.

As I write this, I am sitting in the Sky Room at Delta Airlines in Atlanta, as mechanical problems have forced the delay of my flight from Atlanta to Nashville. As I am out of town on business for four days, I will take the time to write out some priorities for each of our key people in the regular course of business. I have learned to use waiting minutes as best I can, whether in an airline terminal or in a dentist's office. There are approximately thirty separate goals, almost equally divided, to be transmitted to the appropriate executive based on his or her expertise and niche. They will receive a phone call each day from me where conversation will reinforce and emphasize the points I endeavored to make.

For our branch office managers, the most important one or two hours of their week are those invested in the weekly office staff meeting, where they present to the complete sales group. My formula has always been four hours of preparation for one hour of material if it is new. I advise them not to wing it. As the years go by, we can cheat because repetition of a subject becomes new material with an audience after a year-and-a-half has gone by. Interaction is important for any meeting. It is much better to have dialogue than monologue. Getting the audience involved in case study and role play is generally much better than a lecture coming from the person in charge. Participation is the key, and, again, the goal of education is not knowledge, but action. My book, *Hunger, Hutches, and Hustle,* was copied from my weekly newsletters over a period of twenty years of sending out material, culling the best information, and discussing both my successes and failures.

Successful Employees Begin with Successful Leaders

Leadership takes many forms. My branch offices provide leadership on the secondary level for the company. We also have affiliate businesses, such as mortgage, escrow, and title company divisions. In addition, we are involved in making hard-money loans to enable us primarily to create bridge loans and cosmetic repair loans for our customer base.

The highest and best use of my time is to replenish our sales force with fresh blood. In a servicing company based primarily on selling skills, the nature of the business creates turnover. For most of the past fifty years of being in the system, I have never found a written or verbal test that can completely determine an agent's success. We can use various programs to help reduce the amount of speculation, but there is no absolute method. I use two programs that help—the DISC program and the Quadrants program. The two programs establish a reasonable, but not exact, impression of leadership styles.

DISC is an acronym that represents various styles:

- "D" is for Director or Dictator, depending on your point of view.
- "I" represents the Influencer, or the sales personality who operates primarily out of the emotional right side of his or her brain, the logical side incidentally for a minimum amount of time.
- "S" is for the Support person, who is family-oriented and giving.
- "C" represents Compliance. This person operates almost strictly out of the left brain, where analysis can sometimes lead to paralysis.

I perceive myself as having a little S and C, but a great deal of D and healthy amount of I.

The quadrant analysis is another program that gives me some degree of understanding. The Q1 consists of the dominant hostile personality. The Q2 consists of the hostile submissive personality. The Q3 has both submissiveness and warmth, and finally the Q4, the most admirable, is a combination of dominance and warmth. Over the years with growing maturity and age, I have perceived myself as graduating from the dominant hostile to the dominant warm personality, although I could hear different opinions from others who work with me. There are characteristics and beliefs in each of these four quadrant personalities, and a manager with knowledge of this behavior can reflect better and respond based on the personality type.

Characteristics

•Inflexible
•Aggressive
•Highly
  competitive
•Dominates
  discussion
•Overbearing
	•Poor Listener
	•Insensitive
	•Forces his
	  ideas on
	  others
	•Zest for
	  combat
	
	Q1
		•Open
		•Flexible
		•Forceful
		•Good
		  listener
		•Seeks full
		  understanding
		
		Q4
			•Encouraging
			•Empathetic
			•Receptive
			•Assertive
			•Objective about
			  self and others
			•Respects
			  others' ideas

	Q2	**Q3**	•Informal

•Cold
•Disinterested
•Suspicious
•Secretive
•Defensive
•Defeatist
	•Unresponsive
	•Aloof
	•Wary
	•Bleak outlook
	•Pessimistic
	•Distrustful
		•Relaxed
		•Overly
		  friendly
		•Trusting
		•Non-assertive
		•Optimistic
			•Accepts
			  people as
			  they are
			•Sociable
			•Cheerful
			•Appeasing
			•Lacks
			  forcefulness

Beliefs

•It's a dog-eat-dog world
•It's everyone for himself
•You have to stand on your
  own two feet
•Buyers are always resistant
•Selling is a WIN/LOSE
  relationship…Someone has
  to win, someone has to lose
 	
Q1
	•People are self-concerned, but not selfish
	•People buy when their needs are met
	•People are different and need to be
	  understood
	•Selling is a WIN/WIN relationship…I can get
	  what I want by helping others get their
	  needs.
	
	Q4

Q2	**Q3**
•People cannot be trusted, self-serving •People will buy or list whenever they are ready •Persuasion doesn't work •They will contact me when they are ready to sell •Why should I go out of my way for them? •Selling is a LOSE/LOSE relationship •Why should I worry about satisfying their needs…no one worries about me.	•People are basically good •If they like you, they will buy or list with you •The more friends, the better •If people do not treat you well, try to understand their problems •Selling is a LOSE/WIN relationship…having other people's needs met are more important than my needs •I must satisfy others, no matter what the cost to me

165

To be a responsible leader, it is necessary to learn from others. No one has the market cornered on ideas. I attend several seminars a year as a student to network and remain ahead of the trend curve, staying involved with Prudential conventions and conferences and obtaining leadership training. In addition, I belong to a group called Realty Alliance, which consists of seventy of the major realty companies throughout the United States. Our company happens to be sixtieth in the country, based on dollar volume, of 49,000 companies.

Brainstorming with other leaders in the industry gives me more insight. It is a difficult process, but I also reach outside our industry for ideas on how to stay abreast of trends and changes that could affect our company. I copy articles I believe are relevant and topical from *The Realtor*, *The Economist*, *Business Week* magazine, and the *Los Angeles Times* and pass them on to my agents. I am looking for points of view other than mine. You learn and adapt to our business. The key to being a successful and responsible CEO is in both giving and receiving.

As I have joint-venture owners, my leadership has been tempered with compromise. I cannot dictate, nor would I, to someone whom I perceive as an equal in his or her branch office. Persuasion and diplomacy do work; intimidation in the vast majority of communications does not. There is an old expression: a spoonful of honey is worth more than a gallon of vinegar.

Most of the feedback I obtain regarding my performance is informal, but as a joint-venture owner, it is no-holds-barred. A joint-venture owner is not shy and will pick up the phone to communicate with me if there is criticism. I react as best I can to constructive thoughts. I usually ask for a consensus among other executives because my own opinion may not be the best. Seeking advice from others helps a great deal. From time to time, a critique is sent out requesting anonymous feedback, and our outside management coach can bring suggestions directly to my attention.

My personal communication style, as previously mentioned, is to make dozens of phone calls daily and use handwritten notes. I sometimes use e-mail, but I believe the personal touch of a phone call or a personal note is much more effective. I also send out weekly DVDs or CDs on various facets of the profession. Time in my car is spent listening to new CDs that I can pass on to the management team or our sales force. I have constant individual meetings with managers, conduct branch staff meetings, and am available for advanced training.

A CEO's ability to communicate is paramount to his or her success. Toastmasters is a non-profit self-improvement club where you can join at will and combine your efforts with those of others in the club. You normally meet weekly, perhaps for breakfast or lunch, and you compete with each other on the table topics and speeches that are made, and you are judged consistently on various aspects of making a talk. It is extremely rewarding. I had the opportunity, many years ago, to attend Toastmasters every Monday morning at 7 a.m. for five years. There I learned to think and speak on my feet with the five- to seven-minute speeches we were told to make from time to time. We also had to provide our speaking reactions for two minutes on table topics, where a subject was given with no prior preparation. We had to stand on our feet and extemporaneously respond to that subject, and our content and delivery were judged.

One way in which I try to be innovative is when candidates come in for recruitment interviews we give them a book I wrote, and we give six different CDs on various aspects of our company. In addition, we explain the Mulhearn Advantage Programs, where we deliver literally millions of dollars in various programs to help stimulate business by creating transactions the average broker cannot afford to do.

Words of Wisdom for Up-and-Coming Leaders

One of the most important ideas I may have learned about leading a company is a simple "last man standing." I love Will Smith's quote, "If I'm on a treadmill with somebody else, I'll be on that treadmill to the bitter end or die." I will be there when the other person has given up. My obsession is that our business requires courage, high energy, self-discipline, and a sense of urgency.

As CEOs, we wonder whether we actually have the support of our people. It is tough not to be looked upon as a manipulator. No one then really knows for certain whether the CEO is a friend—whether the love is real or is a calculated ploy to take something from them. That is the unfortunate position of being in a leadership role—people will ask themselves if he or she is for real. Who you are eventually shows through. As the old saying goes, "You can fool all the people some of the time, some of the people all the time, but you can't fool all the people all the time."

The greatest lessons of leadership I believe come when you have no choice but to resolve a difficult situation. To handle a loss correctly, you reconsider the methods you used, and you attempt to improve them or change them. The quality and quantity of our performance improves as we practice or as we continue stretching. We need to stretch continuously and decide whether we have enough courage to change and try new ideas.

Key Takeaways

- Decide who you want to be and what you truly want to accomplish in your life, and make the changes you need to do it.
- The best sales people do not always make the best managers.
- Consider SMOST when setting goals: Situation, Mission, Objective, Strategies, and Tactics.
- Good judgment comes with experience, but experience comes from bad judgment.
- Training is critical on every level, but take time especially to develop those with potential who are worth the effort, and always follow through.
- A good mentor teaches by showing, rather than doing.
- To be a successful and responsible leader it is critical to constantly learn from others; no one has the market cornered on ideas.

Bruce T. Mulhearn, is chairman and president of Prudential California Realty, also known as Mulhearn Realtors. Born and educated in England, he immigrated to the United States in 1958 via New Zealand, where he had lived for two years, and settled in Los Angeles.

Mr. Mulhearn obtained his real estate license in 1960, served two years in the US Army, and earned his real estate broker's license in 1964 upon becoming a citizen of the United States. He opened his first real estate office in Bellflower, California, in January

1967. In May 2002, Mr. Mulhearn affiliated his business with Prudential California Realty.

Mr. Mulhearn's other corporations include Castlehead Inc. Escrows and Golden Empire Mortgage Inc. (joint-venture), and he is affiliated with Orange Coast Title, as well.

A passionate believer in the value of education and mentorship, Mr. Mulhearn was an instructor with the California Association of Realtors (CAR) from 1971 to 1985 and has been an instructor with the National Association of Realtors (NAR) from 1974 to the present. He has authored many articles in the CAR publication, California Real Estate magazine, and published four CAR books. He is also the author of Real Estate Office Management for the NAR and Hunger, Hunches & Hustle: An Englishman's 40 Years of Selling Experiences and Misadventures in California Real Estate.

Mr. Mulhearn and his wife, Tomazina, have three children and ten grandchildren. When he is not working or teaching, he enjoys his hobbies, which include snow skiing, bicycling, and swimming.